IMAGES
of America

HOLIDAY WORLD

Bill Koch returned home to Indiana after serving in World War II. His father, Louis J. Koch, had retired from a career as an industrialist and was in the process of opening what would become the world's first theme park. Though Bill initially thought his father's idea was a folly (according to a newspaper account, "I didn't want any part of it"), he quickly saw that Santa Claus Land, with its dedication to the holiday spirit, could be a great place for family fun. Through the years, Bill would use his skills of innovation and marketing in creating a park that appealed to people of all ages and would still be a favorite six decades later. The Pleasureland ride section is pictured here around 1955.

On the cover: Among the most popular attractions in Santa Claus Land's Pleasureland were the hand-pumps cars called the Pump-Its, pictured in the foreground of the photograph. Bill and Pat Koch's five children treasure their memories of riding the Pump-Its. When shown this photograph from his youth, Holiday World president Will Koch remarked, "They were individual cars, not connected. Looks like the person in the front car is going too slow." It was obvious from his tone of voice that he would have been happy to lead the pack. (Courtesy of Holiday World and Splashin' Safari.)

IMAGES
of America

HOLIDAY WORLD

Pat Koch and Jane Ammeson

ARCADIA
PUBLISHING

Published by Arcadia Publishing
Charleston, South Carolina

Library of Congress Catalog Card Number: 2006922107

For all general information contact Arcadia Publishing at:
Telephone 843-853-2070
Fax 843-853-0044
E-mail sales@arcadiapublishing.com
For customer service and orders:
Toll-Free 1-888-313-2665

Visit us on the Internet at www.arcadiapublishing.com

CONTENTS

Acknowledgments

Santa Claus Land and Holiday World and Splashin' Safari are my home, my life, my love. Bill Koch and I formed a team, and together we made a dream come true. As I have grown older with the park, I have realized how important it is to preserve its history in as factual and entertaining a manner as possible. I am indebted to all those who saved and preserved pictures, memorabilia, letters, and other informational materials over more than 60 years.

I owe a special thanks to my mother and father, Jim and Bella Yellig, who kept everything. I am grateful to the Koch family for their preservation of our history. Special acknowledgment to our five children: Will, Kristi, Dan, Philip, and Natalie for their remembrances.

Special thanks to Paula Werne, Joe Hevron, Jerry Sanders, and my wonderful coauthor, Jane Ammeson.

To all who have loved Santa Claus Land and now love Holiday World and Splashin' Safari, I am deeply grateful.

—Pat Koch

When I first met Paula Werne, director of public relations for Holiday World and Splashin' Safari, and Pat Koch and her son Will, who is president of the park, I felt immediately as if I became a part of a warm and wonderful family. Now, years later, I still get that feeling whenever I hear from them or whenever I return to Santa Claus.

—Jane Ammeson

INTRODUCTION

The first theme park in the world is not Disneyland, which opened in 1955, or Six Flags over Texas, which started up six years later. Nor is it in a big city or even a highly populated state. Instead, it is tucked away amidst the rolling hills of southern Indiana in a town called Santa Claus. Premiering in 1946, and originally called Santa Claus Land, Holiday World theme park and Splashin' Safari water park began as the retirement project of Evansville industrialist Louis J. Koch. His son Bill soon became involved and was running the park by the late 1940s, turning it into a family destination that now hosts more than one million visitors a year. Today the next generation of Kochs owns and operates the park.

Well known for family fun, cleanliness, and friendliness, Holiday World and Splashin' Safari are also famed for their wooden roller coasters. Both the Raven and The Legend have repeatedly been ranked among the top wooden coasters on the planet. The park's newest wooden coaster, the Voyage, is predicted to quickly take its place among the world's very best coasters. So how does a small-town theme park become such a hit?

Well, for this third-generation family-owned business, it is all about service, because the Koch family does not see the park as a job or a business but instead as part of their home and their lives.

And how could a park named for a jolly elf not be a magical place? Especially when Santa himself was on hand to spread joy and laughter. And memories. Jim "Santa Jim" Yellig posed for countless photographs over the decades, always with a smile on his face and a twinkle in his eye.

In 1960, Bill Koch married "Santa's daughter," Pat Yellig. Over the next six years, they had five children: Will, Kristi, Dan, Philip, and Natalie. As their family grew, so did the park.

The story of Holiday World and Splashin' Safari is more than that of a successful family business. It is the story of a community, because many of the people who live in and around Santa Claus work (or once worked) at the park, and that sense of family and commitment to common good is reflected in how the park is run.

Repeatedly named the cleanest and friendliest park in the world—beating out Disney World, Kings Island, Busch Gardens, and Cedar Point—Holiday World is the only theme park to offer such a wide range of amenities as free soft drinks, free parking, plus free sunscreen stations throughout Splashin' Safari, which also offers free use of inner tubes. The parks are also smoke-free and promote a family-friendly atmosphere.

It is not unusual to meet people who have worked at the park for decades and whose parents worked there before. Friendships and even marriages have resulted between employees who never ceased to show the true meaning of hospitality to millions of park guests over the years.

Bill Koch passed away several years ago, leaving an enduring legacy, and not just for Holiday World and Splashin' Safari. He built Christmas Lake Village, a family-oriented gated community in Santa Claus; Lake Rudolph Campground and RV Resort; Kringle Place Shopping Center; and much more.

The next generation now owns the park. Will Koch, along with his mother, Pat, continues to take great pride in the high standards his family set long ago, which his employees continue to emulate each day.

"We never want to lose that small-park feel," Will Koch explains. "No matter how many guests we serve and how big we grow. The key is our steadfast adherence to the values established long ago as our park's cornerstones: safety, service, cleanliness, and friendliness."

One

IN THE BEGINNING

SANTA CLAUS, INDIANA

With no stoplights, no paved roads, and no electricity until 1940, Santa Claus may have looked like a sleepy rural southern Indiana town, but Louis J. Koch saw potential in this small town with the world-famous name. Through the years he, his son Bill, and other Koch children and grandchildren would put the tiny town on the map. The Koch family was among a number of entrepreneurs who were determined to make Santa Claus a place where Christmas was celebrated year-round.

Originally the town, which was laid out in 1846, was named Santa Fe. After it was determined there already was a Santa Fe, Indiana, the town's leaders had to agree on another name. On Christmas Eve 1992, radio news commentator Paul Harvey recalled on his show *The Rest of the Story* how this small town became Santa Claus. The story begins with the townsfolk sitting around a potbellied stove on Christmas Eve night in 1852, discussing what to name the town. The circuit-riding minister, Rev. Christian Wyttenbach, was there, having just conducted the Christmas Eve service. Someone suggested that Wyttenbach sounded like a good name. Reverend Wyttenbach reportedly declined the honor, and while the discussion went on, a burst of cold winter air blew the church door open and, according to Harvey, "beyond the picture-framed doorway was a magical scene of snowflakes winking on black velvet and the magical sound of sleigh bells." The children, who had been sitting quietly in the room while the adults discussed the town's name, ran to the door shouting, "Santa Claus! Santa Claus!" Suddenly the decision of what to name the town became simple. On May 21, 1856, the name of Santa Claus was accepted by the United States Post Office Department.

Early on, people who traveled to Santa Claus hoping to see Santa were disappointed that he was not there. That was why Evansville industrialist Louis J. Koch decided to create Santa Claus Land. Buying the land for the park, he envisioned a place where children (and adults) could celebrate Christmas no matter what time of the year. Today multiple generations of the Koch family are still an integral part of Santa Claus and the joy the town has brought to millions of families over the span of six decades.

Joe Hevron, age six, sits on a bench in downtown Santa Claus in this photograph taken in 1935. Hevron started working at Santa Claus Land when he was 15 and is still on their staff, coming to work every day. His history with the theme park reflects the continuity and community that define Holiday World and Splashin' Safari.

Santa Claus could have just been another small town, albeit one with a memorable name. However, the Koch family saw much more beyond the dirt roads of this small Hoosier town, which now hosts more than a million visitors to Holiday World and Splashin' Safari each year. "I remember my father saying that the town is named Santa Claus and that there should be something more for children here," recalls Katheryne Bosse, daughter of Louis J. Koch. "Christmas was important in our house, and I remember waking up on Christmas mornings and seeing the big old-fashioned German Christmas tree with candles on it. My father would set up a train in the living room, and we had all types of mechanized things like ice-skaters on the pond and a Ferris wheel in the living room on Christmas Day."

The first Santa Claus Post Office building stood on what is now the intersection of State Road 245 and State Road 162, near where the American Legion now stands. John Specht, who had been the postmaster in Rockport, Indiana, was the first postmaster of Santa Claus, according to Jerry Sanders, park archivist. Specht first wrote "Santa Clause" on the application to the post office (in an interesting aside, Santa Fe was originally misspelled as Santa Fee). Specht's salary was $17.85 per year, and the post office's income in 1856 was $7.29. In 1946, this building was moved to Santa Claus Land; it is now the Betsy Ross Doll House in the Holiday Fourth of July section.

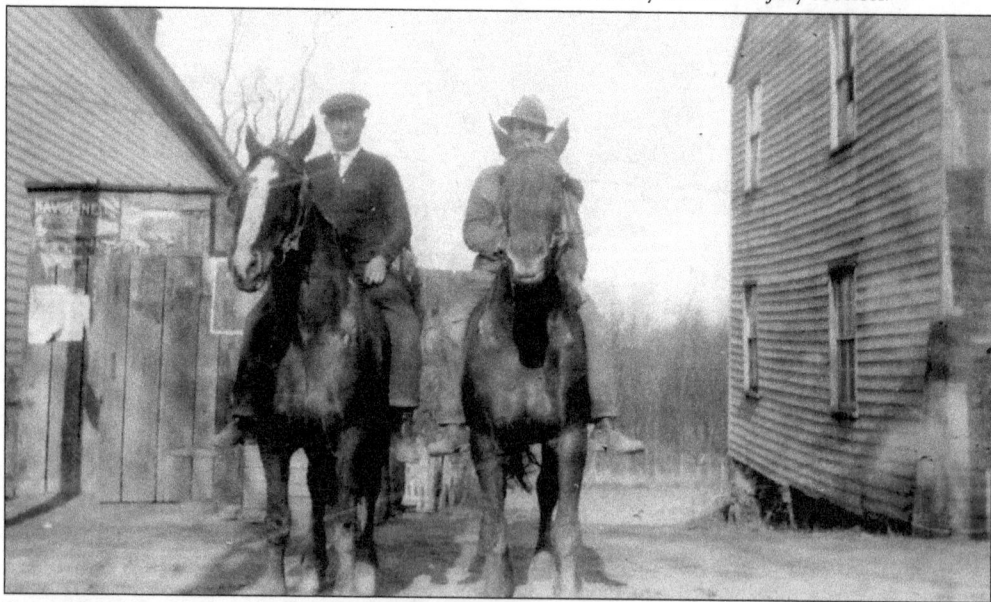

Postmaster James Martin is on the left between the James Martin General Merchandising Store and the Santa Claus Hotel and Restaurant. According to Jerry Sanders, park archivist, James's father, Louis Martin, was the town's 13th postmaster (from 1903 to 1914), and James worked as his assistant, taking over on May 18, 1914. He would officially hold the job until April 30, 1935, even though he died on April 27; his family and assistants performed the postmaster duties until a new postmaster was appointed.

It was James Martin who began promoting the Santa Claus postmark in 1914 when, at his own expense, he began mailing response letters from Santa to children who mailed their Christmas lists to Santa Claus, Indiana. According to Jerry Sanders, park archivist, it was around this time that other post offices started the "courtesy custom" of forwarding the thousands of letters addressed to Santa to the Santa Claus Post Office. They would do so even when the letters did not have a stamp on them.

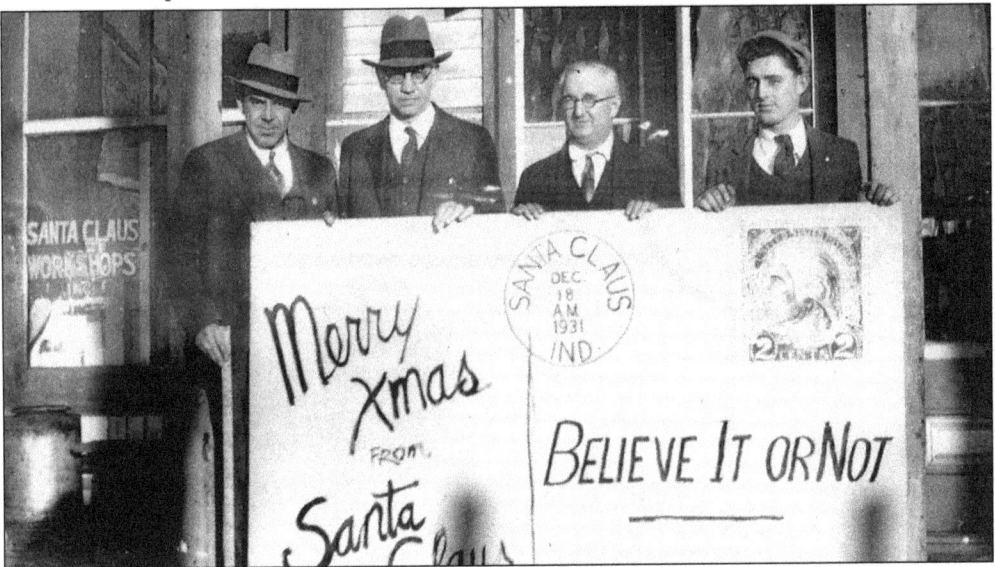

"Commercial interest in Santa Claus, Indiana, probably began when Robert Ripley of 'Believe It or Not' featured the town's post office and postmaster," writes Jerry Sanders, park archivist. That same year, 1930, Congressman Harry Rowbottom of Indiana introduced a bill in the U.S. House of Representatives providing more pay for the postmaster of Santa Claus. This postcard, said to be the largest ever mailed in the world, was sent from New York to Santa Claus during the week of December 12, 1931. It was canceled with a Santa Claus postmark and sent back. Martin is the third man from the left in this photograph.

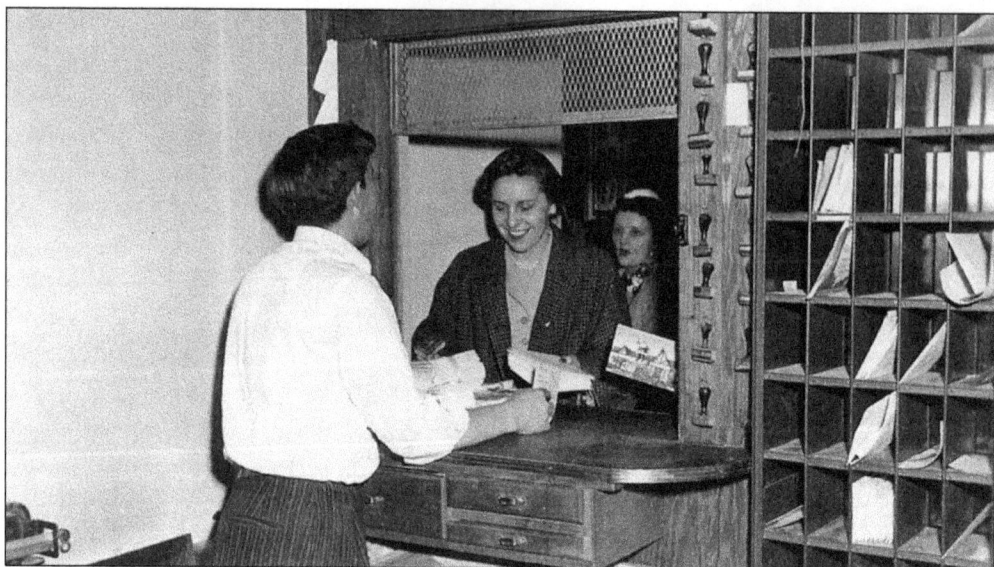

Postmaster James Martin told his friend Jim Yellig that the *Ripley's Believe It or Not* cartoon had increased the amount of mail from children to such an extent that he could no longer answer it all, says Jerry Sanders, park archivist. Jim and his wife, Isabelle, began answering all the letters that had a return address. This further increased the amount of letters that children sent to Santa. "We thought every letter deserved an answer, but the mail soon became too much for us to handle," Yellig said. Later that year, two mailing machines capable of postmarking 40,000 letters an hour were sent to Santa Claus.

In 1932, the U.S. postmaster suggested that the name of Santa Claus be changed to something else to stop the blizzard of Christmas mail. According to Jerry Sanders, that suggestion aroused residents not only of Indiana but around the country to protest. Rep. John W. Boehne vowed to stay in Washington, D.C., to fight the name change, stating, "Consideration must be given to those youngsters who profess the faith in a Santa Claus. . . . Do not destroy this faith by a ruthless order of your department." The attempt failed, and Santa Claus remained the town's name.

This photograph was taken in front of the Santa Claus Post Office in 1933, the same year that the Santa Claus American Legion was founded. Many of the legion members began to help answer the children's letters to Santa at the urging of James Martin, Jim Yellig, and others.

The Santa Claus American Legion played an integral part in the development of the town and ultimately the theme park as legionnaires volunteered to answer the hundreds of thousands of letters that flowed into the small-town post office. Here, in this 1939 photograph, is an American Legion ceremony. The man in the front row wearing an American Legion uniform centered between the two American flags is Jim Yellig. The man in the uniform third to the right of Yellig is Orville Martin from Rockport, Indiana, a dedicated supporter of the Santa Claus American Legion. Yellig was the first commander of the Santa Claus American Legion. The Dale High School Band is on the right.

Santa Jim Yellig supervises while a helpful elf paints the mailbox at the Santa Claus Post Office.

American Legion members sit in Kaiser Drugstore in Dale, Indiana, five miles northwest of Santa Claus, sorting through letters and looking like they are having a good time. From left to right are Elbert Reinke, who was postmaster of Santa Claus from 1947 to 1973; Floyd Kaiser, the owner of the drugstore; Glenn Guth; Jack Winkler; and Roy Ferguson Jr. One of the letters they received was from Linda Rouse of Shepherdsville, Kentucky, and read, "I am seven years old and I've made 14 A's on my report card." Nancy Lee Gordon told Santa, "I will leave you cookies and milk, as I did last Christmas."

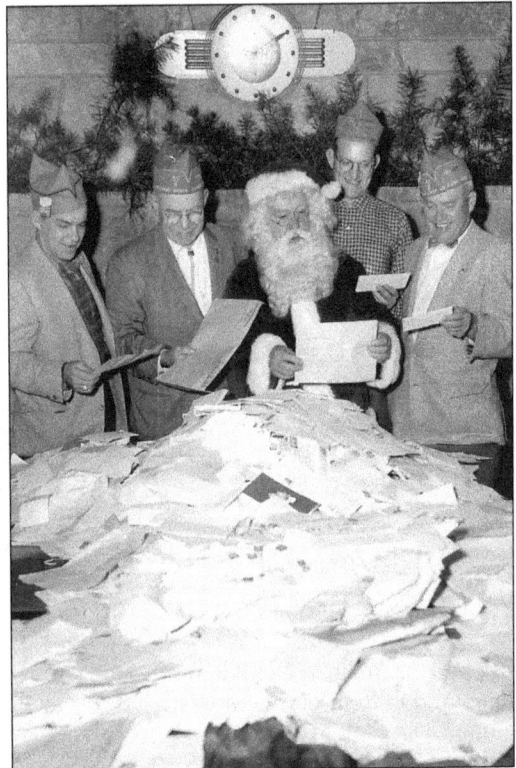

Mail continued to arrive. In 1957, according to park archivist Jerry Sanders, the Santa Claus Post Office received approximately five million pieces of mail. That accounts for about 79,366 letters for each of the town's 63 residents. From left to right are Elbert Reinke, Roy Fenn, Santa Jim Yellig, Bill Winkler, and an unidentified friend.

As the town's fame grew, several businessmen saw the potential in developing Santa Claus into a tourist destination. One of these entrepreneurs was Carl Barrett, who built a Santa Claus statue and opened the Santa Claus Park in 1935. The Santa statue, which weighs 40 tons and is 22 feet tall, took 350 bags of concrete to make; it is still standing in its original location just southeast of Holiday World on State Road 245. Barrett is the man bending over on the left side of the statue. This photograph was taken at the statue's dedication, attended by a reported 1,000 people, just a few days before Christmas. The dedication ceremony was covered by radio station WGBF of Evansville, Indiana. It was necessary to run a special transmission wire to Louisville and Evansville for the broadcast.

Ray and Pat Yellig, the children of Jim, stand in front of the statue in Santa Claus Park in a photograph taken in the late 1930s.

Because the American Legion participated in answering the letters to Santa Claus, legionnaires from all over came to Santa Claus. This photograph shows J. L. Lowman of American Legion Post No. 242 (the Santa Claus American Legion Post) in front of the Santa Claus statue with his bird, Pete. On the back is handwritten, "Pete and I are going to start South tomorrow. God bless you, Jim [meaning Jim Yellig]. You have helped me a lot."

Attorney Milton Harris was another entrepreneur who saw the commercial viability of a town named Santa Claus. He built the St. Nicholas Castle and Old Curiosity Shop, which was commonly called the Candy Castle, pictured here in the 1970s. In 1936, according to park archivist Jerry Sanders, Harris also began work on the Toy Land Enchanted Forest where he leased space to at least seven companies, including Lionel Trains, Daisy Air Rifles, and Buddy "L" Trucks.

This photograph of the Candy Castle was taken on Memorial Day in 1939.

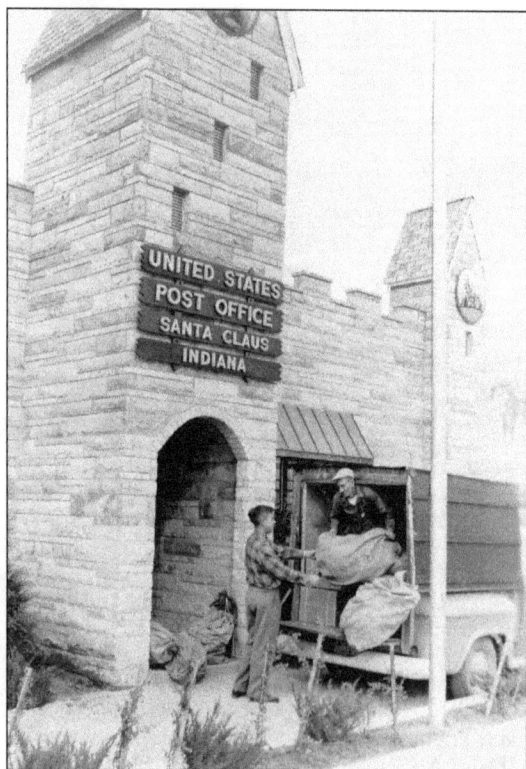

The mail continued to increase each year. Postmaster Elbert Reinke helps unload mail at the Santa Claus Post Office in this picture taken in the late 1950s. In 1949, 30 people lived in Santa Claus according to information provided by Jerry Sanders, park archivist.

Pat Koch recalls that her father, Jim Yellig, often had her perform at special occasions including this Memorial Day service in the 1940s. Jim, out of his Santa suit and wearing his military uniform, is on her right. He served in the U.S. Navy from 1913 to 1931, having enlisted at the age of 19.

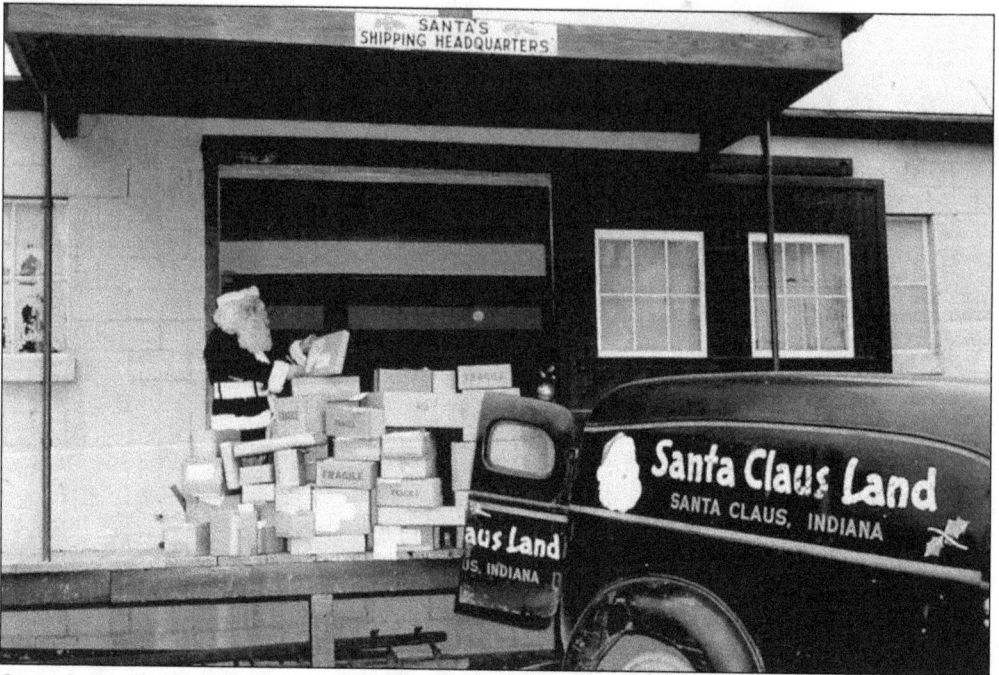

Santa Jim Yellig looks at the mail as it arrives at Santa's Shipping Headquarters in this c. 1946 photograph. Jerry Sanders, park archivist, recounts some of the funniest letters, including "Santa, please don't tell mommy and daddy we burned down the garage!" and "Santa, we don't have a chimney but mommy always leaves the back door unlocked." There was even a young girl from Japan who wrote, "Dear Santa, we don't have a chimney. Please don't eat our food."

In 1946, 25¢ got a child a Christmas letter from Santa, including the cost of a 3¢ stamp.

The Santa Claus Post Office is seen here in 1964, the year it was torn down. Standing in front of the post office is Gil Fahr, a longtime employee at Santa Claus Land and friend to Bill Koch.

The Santa Claus Post Office was located inside Santa Claus Land from October 5, 1947, to the fall of 1957.

Restored Original Santa Claus Post Office 1856, Santa Claus, Ind.

Here is a postcard showing the original Santa Claus Post Office after it had been restored.

Store and Post Office at Santa Claus, Ind.

This 1960s postcard of the second Santa Claus Post Office includes a view of the large Santa Claus Headquarters sign and an old gas pump in front.

This Santa Claus Post Office, located next to Santa Claus Land's front gate, opened in 1957.

Today the town includes Kringle Place, which features the Santa Claus Post Office, Santa Claus Museum, and other commercial venues. Most of Kringle Place is owned by Philip Koch and Kristi Koch George, who are also the owners of Lake Rudolph Campground and RV Resort.

This barn sits on property owned by Willis Reinke, who was the brother of Elbert, one of the Santa Claus postmasters. The barn was built in the 1880s. The lobby of the popular Santa's Lodge in Santa Claus was built using the original wooden beams from the barn. (Photograph courtesy of Mary Jane Brittingham, a good friend of the Yellig family who worked at Santa Claus Land during its first season.)

Santa's Lodge is decorated for Christmas both inside and out throughout the year. The lodge overflows with guests during the months that Holiday World and Splashin' Safari are open. (Photograph courtesy of Santa's Lodge.)

Two

SANTA CLAUS LAND

Santa Claus Land opened on August 3, 1946, becoming the first theme park in the world. Founder Louis J. Koch bought the land for the park in the 1930s. A year after World War II ended, the park, with Santa Jim Yellig, was ready to open. John Long, husband of Bill Koch's sister, Martha Lois, remembers being there on that first day. "It was crowded," he says. "It was a great day for the family."

Louis J. Koch, known as "Mr. Louie" to his family, friends and employees, is pictured here with his wife, Clarice. Louis, a leading industrialist from nearby Evansville, Indiana, founded Santa Claus Land as a retirement project. As the father of nine children, he had firsthand experience of the great joy Santa Claus and Christmas can bring to children's lives. A shortage of labor and materials during World War II did not prevent him from fulfilling his dream; it just postponed it for a while. On August 4, 1945, ground was broken for the park, which would open the following year.

Louis J. Koch's middle son, Bill, began operating the park in 1948; a decade later, he was named president of Santa Claus Land. Constantly searching for creative rides and attractions, he told a reporter, "Even though we weren't the biggest park, we wanted to make it the best."

Louis J. Koch was a train aficionado; he hired Ted Buehn, a model train enthusiast, to build this 1/8th scale train based on a Baltimore and Ohio locomotive. Constructed at the family's Evansville business, George Koch Sons, the Santa Claus Land Railroad was the first ride in the park. Now called the Freedom Train, its popularity continues, six decades later. Driving the train is Santa Jim, whose daughter, Pat, married Bill Koch in 1960. Three of Pat and Bill's five children still own and operate the park. "Grandpa Louie had this train made, and it was brought up here and running the park's first season," says Pat Koch, who rode the train frequently when she was young. "It's been a favorite ever since."

Several years ago, a man corresponded with the park, reminiscing that he had visited Santa Claus Land and ridden the train with his grandfather many years before. According to Paula Werne, director of public relations for the park, his e-mail ended with the news that just that day he had ridden the same train with his granddaughter. "Five generations!" marvels Paula. "We tell that story to our hosts and hostesses to help them comprehend how important their jobs are. We're part of families' precious memories."

This early rides area at Santa Claus Land is now "back of the house" at Holiday World. Many of the park's directors have offices in the original building that once housed a restaurant and shops.

Louis J. Koch liked trains so much that he had one in the backyard at his home in Evansville. The Santa Claus Land Railroad became the Mother Goose Land Train in the 1950s, as it wound its way past nursery rhymes made by Lewis Sorensen from Los Angeles.

"I still enjoy seeing the Mother Goose figures when I go home to visit the park," says Dan Koch, middle son of Pat and Bill. Though the figures date back to the 1950s, they still delight children—and adults—today. Dan remembers the train as being one of his favorite rides in the park. Of his father, he remembers, "how hard he worked but how he always had time for his children, too."

"The Pioneer Land Train looped around the park past nursery-rhyme statues, and the conductor would stop and narrate stories about what we were seeing, including the Lincoln homestead in the Pioneer Village," says Rick Emmons, who visited the park as a boy and has now worked as the park's graphic artist for 30 years. "I never expected the park to grow as big as it has," he says. "It's almost overwhelming."

31

There were other ways to see the park in addition to the trains. In this photograph, Walter Reinke drives visitors in an old stagecoach that dates back to the late 1800s. According to Joe Hevron, a longtime park employee, the coach originally was used to pick up passengers at the Southern Railroad depot in nearby Dale, Indiana, and take them to Wahl's Hotel in Dale back around the beginning of the 20th century. The park bought the coach, refurbished it, and turned it into a popular attraction.

For years, many of the roads in the park were unpaved. Here horses pull the old stagecoach through a scenic area in Santa Claus Land.

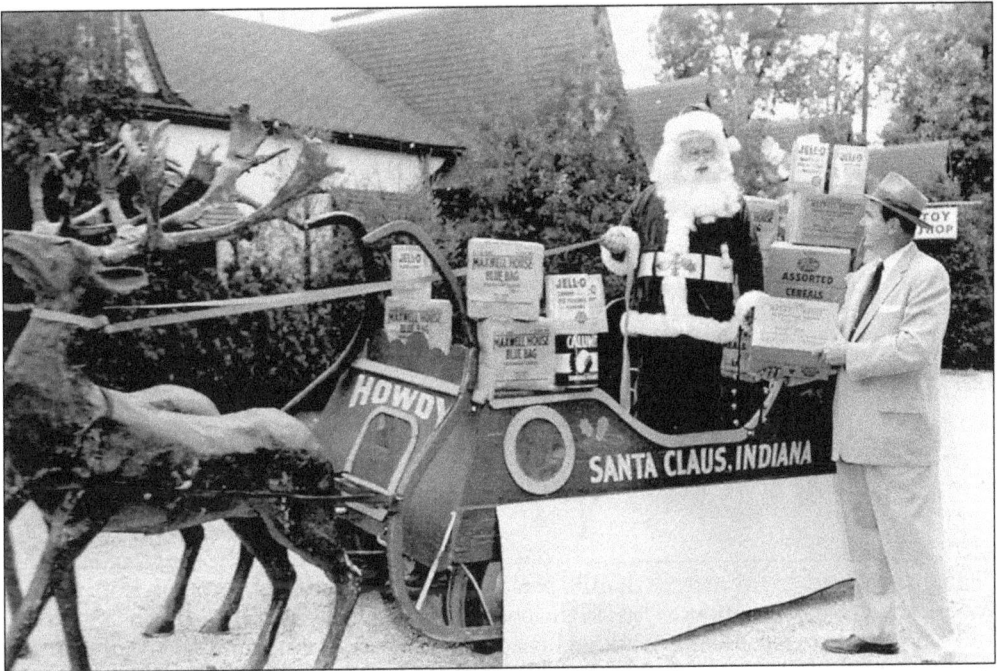

Santa Jim Yellig was so popular that he was frequently featured in advertisements. Here he loads up on boxes of Jell-O.

The Tour Train with its "futuristic" styling was a popular ride in the 1970s. This train, which was bright red, is fondly remembered by the Koch children. "All five of our children worked here from the time they were about ten," Bill told a newspaper reporter in 2000. "As youngsters they played elves and dwarves. As they grew, so did their responsibilities." Bill and Pat encouraged their children to go on all the rides and provide feedback about their likes and dislikes.

Santa Jim Yellig took part in more than 30 parades across the country for both state and national American Legion conventions. This sleigh appeared in parades as far away as Miami, St. Louis, and Los Angeles. According to park archivist Jerry Sanders, American Legions all over the country contributed to the cost of making the papier-mache reindeer shown here. In an amusing story that Santa Jim loved to tell, the reindeer were put in a railroad car and shipped to Miami for a parade. Several people misunderstood, thinking them to be real reindeer and complained loudly that the animals were not getting food or water.

This 1950s photograph shows Santa Jim in an old-time sleigh that is still on exhibit in the Toy Museum at Holiday World.

One of the many signs that have welcomed people to the park over the years, this one dates back to the 1950s.

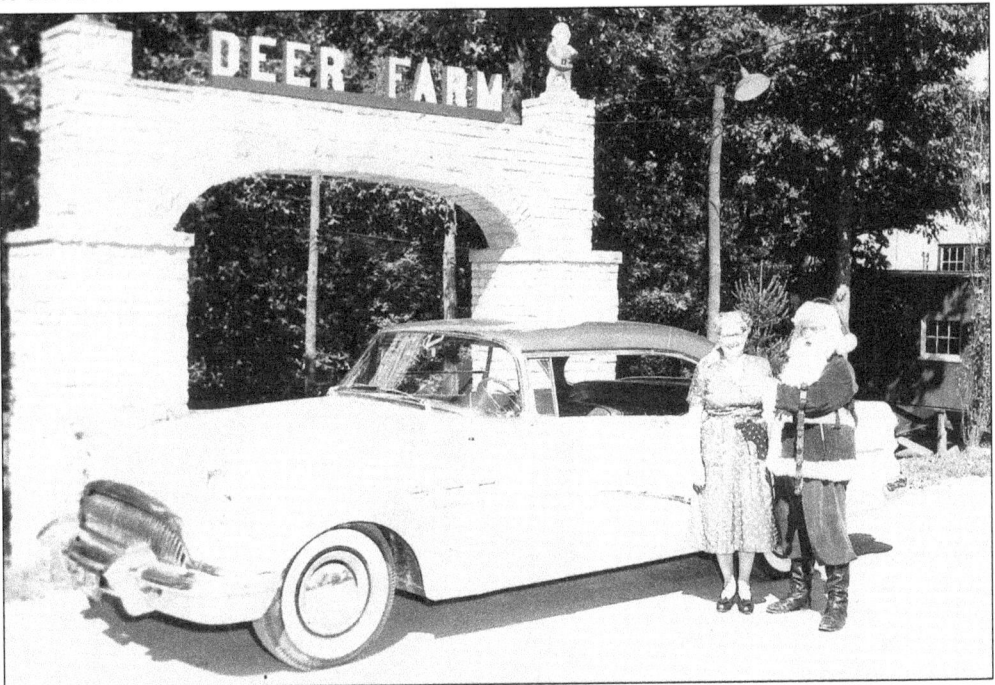

Proving he did not always travel by rail or sleigh, Santa Jim stands with his wife, Isabelle, in front of a brand new Dodge. In the background is the entrance to the Deer Farm, which opened in 1948 and was a popular attraction at the park for several decades.

Santa Jim Yellig visits the Deer Farm at Santa Claus Land. At one time the farm had 14 European white fallow deer as well as several peacocks. Will Koch, president of Holiday World, recalls that children could purchase deer food pellets and reach through the fence to feed them. Mary Jane Brittingham, who worked at the park when she was a teenager, remembers that in 1947, one of the does was born on her birthday, July 2.

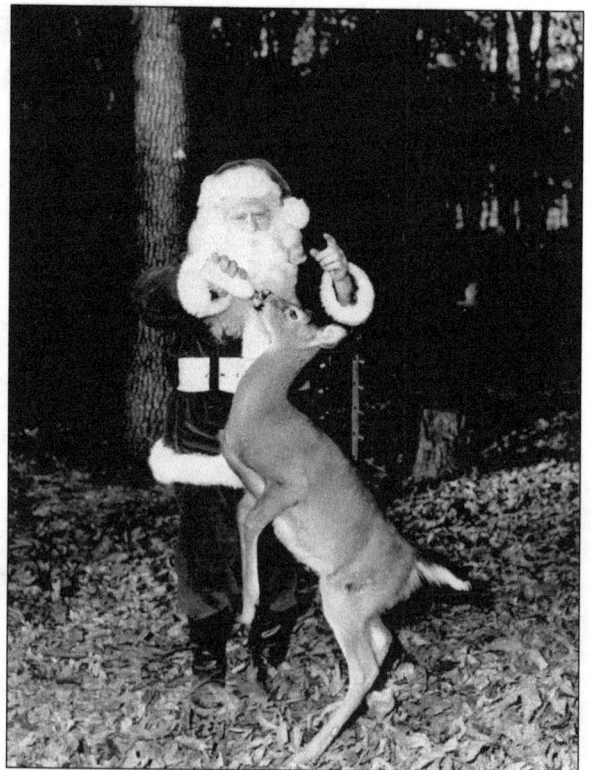

Santa Jim tends to a deer at the Deer Farm in Santa Claus Land. The first deer were named Donner, Blitzen, Comet, and Cupid. Bill Koch liked telling the story of when the original deer arrived a few days late. "We handed out flyers that said, 'Oh, dear! No deer!' and invited visitors to come back and see the deer free of charge."

The Educated Animal shows were a big attraction at the Deer Farm. Here the Kissing Bunny gives a big smooch to his plastic counterpart. It must have been quite a kiss, as she lit up afterward. The animals, which came from a company based in Hot Springs, Arkansas, were trained by Keller Breland, owner of Animal Behavior Enterprises, who used operant conditioning to teach the animals tricks. Their food was reward for performing.

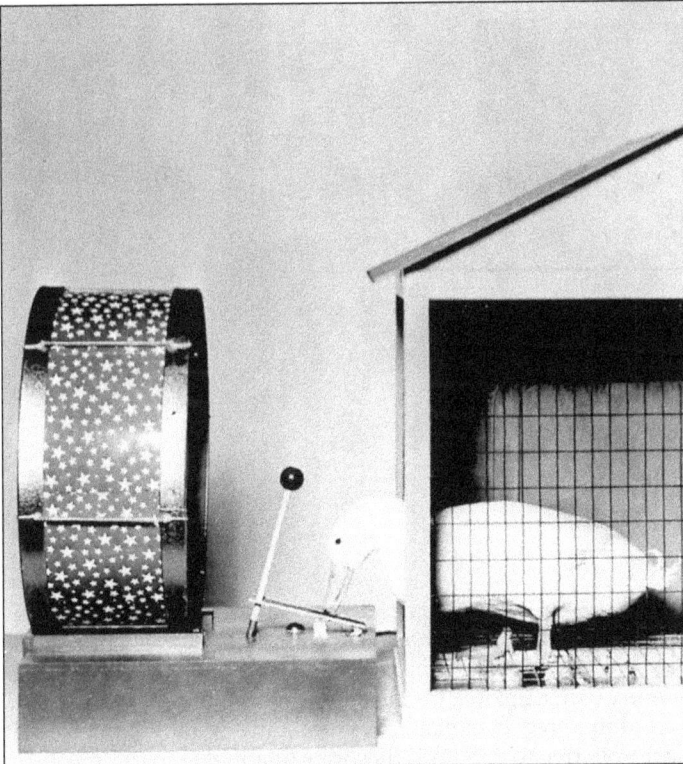

The Drumming Duck plays music in a favorite attraction at Santa Claus Land. Will Koch, president of Holiday World and Splashin' Safari, worked with the animals when he was in his early teens. "We had to have extra animals since once an animal had eaten enough, he wouldn't perform anymore," recalls Koch.

Not all the Educated Animals performed in the Deer Farm. The Fire Chief Rabbit had his own kiosk near what is now the Freedom Train's station. The park's graphic artist, Rick Emmons, remembers that one of his jobs was feeding the animals. "My favorite was the baseball chicken," he says. "It would hit a home run and then run around the bases—that is, if it hadn't eaten too much."

The macaws were also part of the Educated Animals and were quite expensive, about $12,000 each, in the early 1970s. Will Koch recalls one time a macaw's wing was clipped improperly and it managed to fly away. "Almost every park employee went looking for that macaw," recalls Will, who notes the bird was finally spied in a tree. Park employees took turns watching the bird for more than three days, following it from tree to tree until they were finally able to capture it.

Will Koch started working at the park when he was 10. His earliest job was to dress up in costumes. His second job was to manage the Punch and Judy Show; a chicken played Miss Judy, and a rabbit was Professor Punch. Koch trained Punch to jump through a hoop and Judy to pull Punch out of a hat. "Punishment was never used in training these animals," recalls Koch.

Ronald Reagan, who hosted a television program called *General Electric Theater*, stopped by the park in March 1955 after visiting a General Electric plant in nearby Tell City, Indiana. Later that year, Disneyland opened, and Reagan became their spokesperson. Pictured with him are Santa Jim Yellig and Louis J. Koch. Helen Koch Robb, one of Bill Koch's sisters, shared her memories of that visit. "Mr. Reagan was a very gracious gentleman and seemed to enjoy his trip very much," she recalled in 1980. "He was about 45 years old at this time and Dad was 73 years old. Times change and now this same Mr. Reagan will be inaugurated as the fortieth president of the United States on January 20, 1981."

On January 10, 1962, Bill Koch was present when Pres. John F. Kennedy signed legislation creating the Lincoln Boyhood National Memorial in nearby Lincoln City, Indiana. Witnessing the signing are, from left to right, Congressman Fred Schwengel of Iowa; Isadora Skora, a Lincoln scholar from Evansville, Indiana; Sen. Vance Hartke of Indiana; Bill Koch; Roy T. Combs, president of the Indiana Lincoln Foundation; and Congressman Winfield K. Denton of Evansville. Pat Koch still remembers feeling honored when President Kennedy crossed the Oval Office to present her with the last pen that had been used in the signing.

In another project that benefited his community, Bill Koch was instrumental in creating a grassroots effort in the 1960s to persuade the federal government to improve the planned route for Interstate 64, bringing it farther south in Indiana. "We joke that Bill's favorite hobby was highways," says Pat Koch. Gov. Frank O'Bannon was on hand in 2002 as three generations of Kochs helped dedicate the renaming of Indiana Highway 162 between I-64 and Lincoln City the William A. Koch Memorial Highway.

In 1958, Santa Claus Land included 240 acres, had its own lake, campground, five miles of roads and walkways, and published its own quarterly newspaper.

This wide-mouthed whale stood in the center of the park at Santa Claus Land. The whale was created by Lewis Sorensen, who also made the wax figures for the park's Hall of Famous Americans and the Native American statues for the park's Pioneer Village.

One of the few classic "flying scooter" rides still around, Eagle's Flight was added to the park in 1976, the same year the entrance to Santa Claus Land was relocated from State Road 162 to State Road 245.

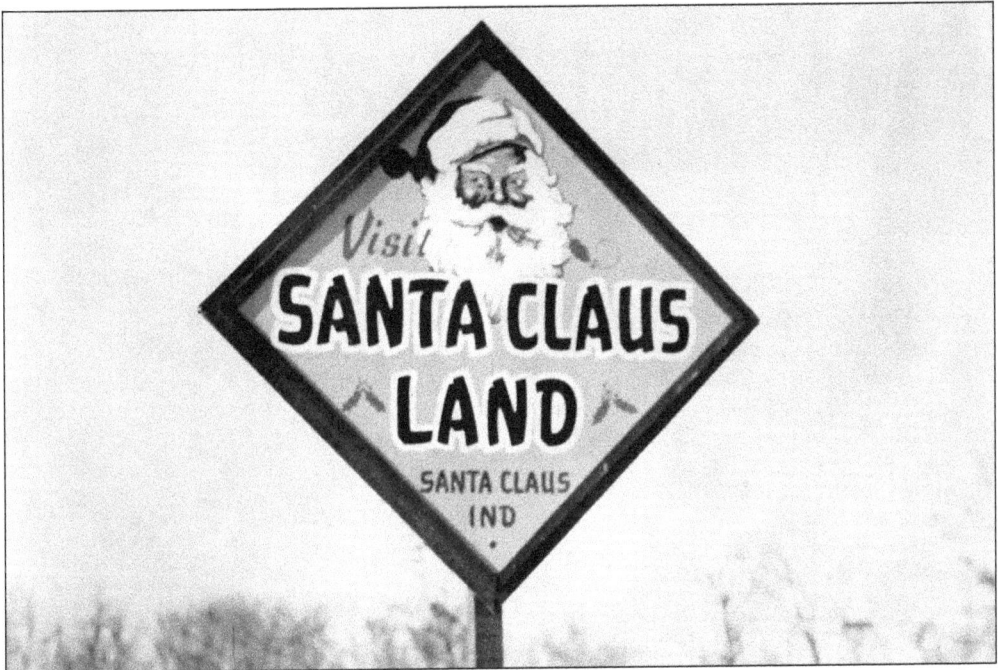

Signs inviting visitors to come to Santa Claus Land were posted along many of the winding country roads throughout southern Indiana. This sign dates back to the 1950s.

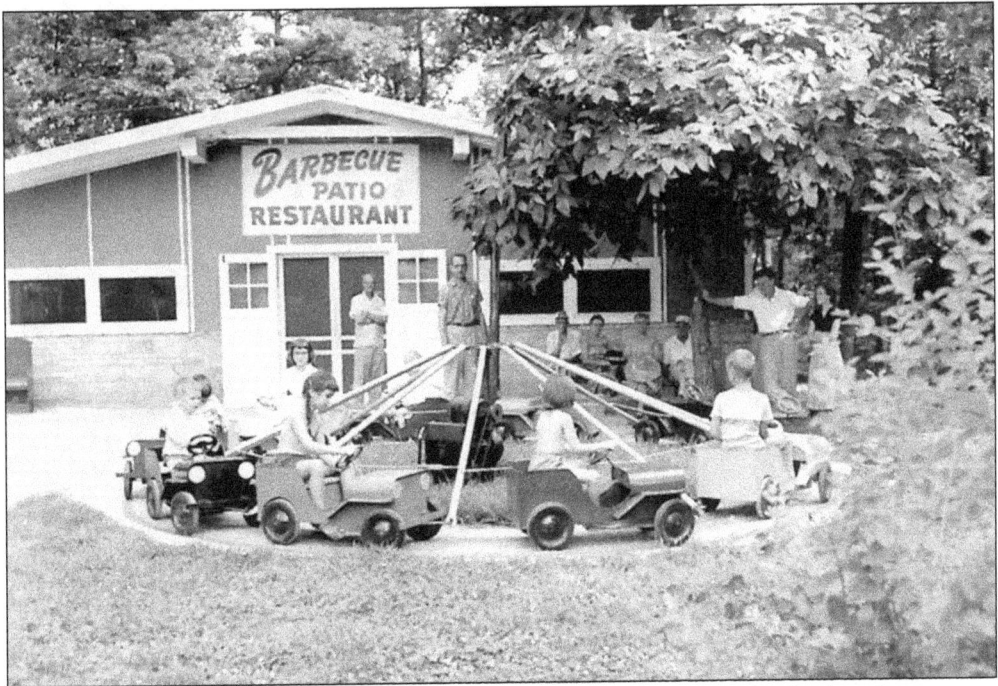

The Jeep-Go-Round, added to Santa Claus Land in 1947, was the first of its kind in the country.

The Miniature Circus was part of the park from 1946 until the mid-1970s. Longtime park employee Rick Emmons remembers the circus as one of his favorite attractions when he visited Santa Claus Land as a young boy. "It was something you could look at for a long time because there was so much to see," he says. "It had moving figures, including a trainer who pulled an elephant."

Here is another view of the Miniature Circus at Santa Claus Land. Frieda Foertsch, who has worked at the park for 51 years, painted the tents and the characters and says the tents went up like real tents.

The Lewis and Clark Trail ride was added to the park in 1978. Within the next four years, several more rides were added, including Thunder Bumpers on Chesapeake Bay and Dancer's Thunder Bumpers Junior. The family got many of their ideas for rides by visiting other theme and amusement parks. "Vacations were spent at other theme parks across the country, making comparisons and gathering ideas," Bill Koch told a reporter in 2000.

This photograph ran in a December 1958 newspaper article that recounted a nation-wide contest held by the Santa Claus Chamber of Commerce searching for children who had been born on Christmas Day. Bill Koch congratulates the two winners, Hilton Reeves from Mount Vernon, Indiana, and Michael Langenfield from Hastings, Minnesota. Reeves, the boy in the black cowboy hat, invited all those he met to "visit Posey County, home of the famous watermelon patches and where the Ohio River blows a breeze of freshness."

According to a press release dated December 10, 1959, "10-year-old Sharon Gentner of Akron, Ohio, will reign December 13 as honorary mayor of Santa Claus, Indiana, and Linda Belle Lipsey of New Albany, Indiana, will assist as honorary police chief. A committee of four judges from the Santa Claus Chamber of Commerce selected the winners from thousands of letters. Sharon wrote that, 'It would be a great honor because Santa Claus town must be a town of love because Santa loves all children so much.' Sharon, a fourth grader at St. Peter's School in Akron, will serve as Santa's assistant and wear a red velvet and white fur costume. Climaxing the event will be a Christmas Birthday Dinner for Sharon, who will be 11 on Christmas Day, and Linda, who will be 11 on Christmas Eve."

46

Three

THE LITTLE PARK
THAT COULD

The Willie Bartley Ski Thrill Team was a big hit at Santa Claus Land. Bartley and some members of the team were from Ferdinand, a small town about 10 miles northeast of Santa Claus. This photograph shows the Flag Salute, the opening act of the water show, which ran seven days a week. The woman holding the flag is Joy Milligan from Madisonville, Kentucky.

Santa Jim Yellig poses with members of the Willie Bartley Ski Thrill Team. The woman on the far left is Frances Quante from Ferdinand, who skied at Florida's Cypress Gardens in the winter. Next to her is Joy Milligan from Madisonville, Kentucky. The team performed on Lake Rudolph for three summers starting in 1959. According to longtime employee Joe Hevron, even though Lake Rudolph was small, the towboat had two 100-horsepower engines that could accelerate rapidly so that the teams could perform their stunts.

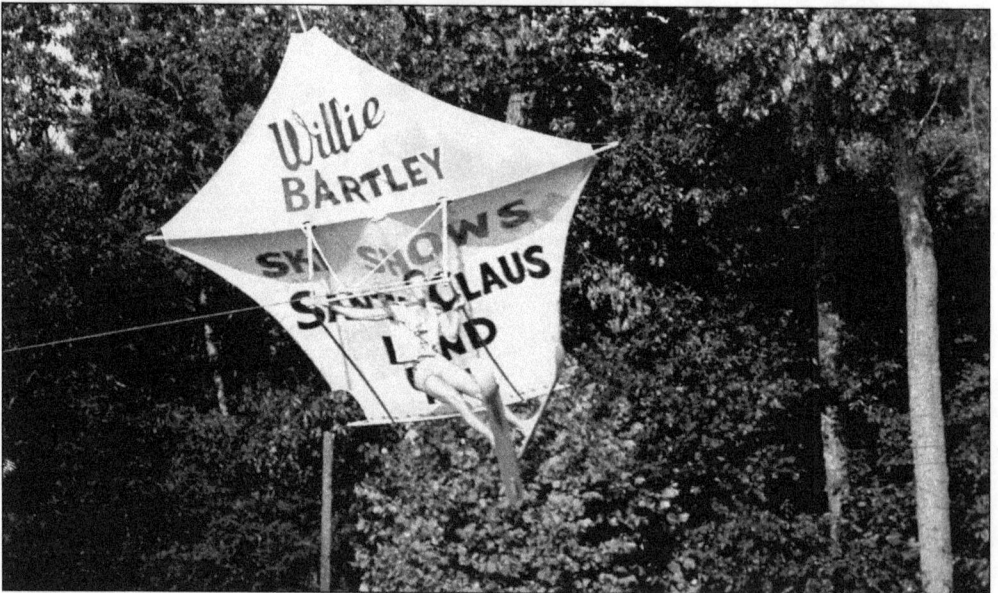

Willie Bartley had served in the National Guard and had traveled to the Wisconsin Dells where he saw water shows, according to his widow, Vita, who still lives in Ferdinand and works seasonally at the park. He came home with the idea of doing the same thing on Lake Rudolph. "Everyone wanted to be in the show," remembers Vita, who designed the costumes for the performers, including sewing sequins on the opera-length gloves that the women wore so that they sparkled in the sunlight.

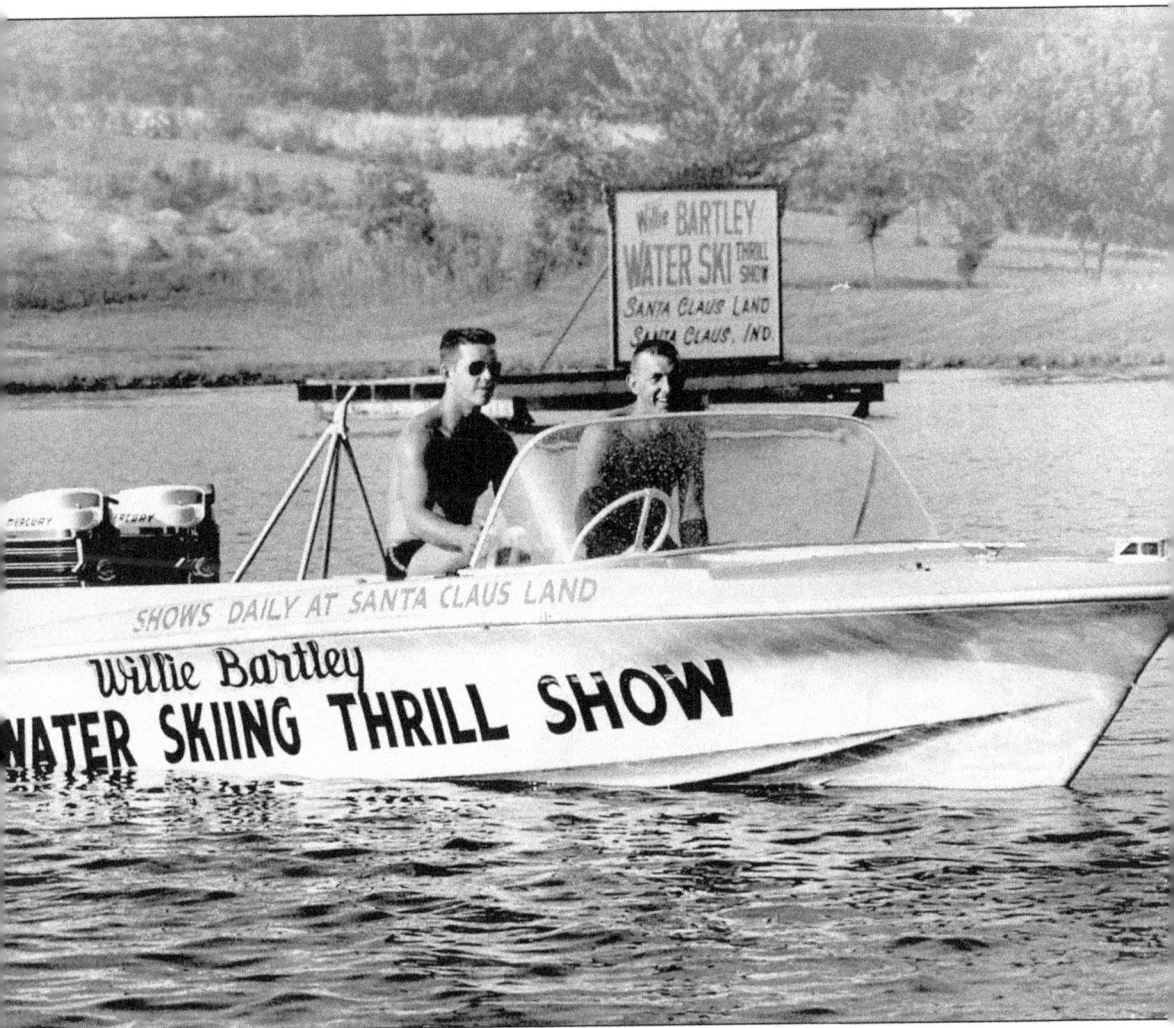

One of the more unusual Santa Claus Land promotions took place on September 4, 1960. According to Jerry Sanders, park archivist, George Jackson, a professional water-skier with the show, set a world's record by skiing 2,000 miles from Santa Claus to Tampa, Florida. Their route took the Santa Claus Jet Boat Special down nearby Crooked Creek to the Ohio River, and from there to the Mississippi River to the Gulf Water Coastal Waterways to the Gulf of Mexico, and then on to Tampa. Jerry Krampe, 22, of Ferdinand, drove the boat.

According to magician Art Bausman, who worked with Gene Smith (left) and Happy Kellems, Smith was a tap dancer and magician whose motto was Feats of Hands and Feats of Feet. "The Showboat Theatre was great," recalls Philip Koch. "I used to love watching the vaudeville acts of magician Arte Williams and clown, Happy Kellems. I remember skipping rocks in that fountain with Happy Kellems." (Photograph courtesy of Art Bausman.)

Magician Art Bausman performs one of his magic shows on the Santa Claus Land Showboat. Bausman, whose stage name was Arte Williams, worked at the park for a decade. His wife, Pat, had a puppet show at the park. Bausman describes working at the park as the best job he has ever had.

Performers sing and dance at the Hoosier Hoedown in 1978 at the park's country music show.

Decorations remained on Santa Claus Land's 70-foot Christmas tree year-round. Park president Will Koch remembers playing King of the Hill on the mound where the tree stood with other members of the Santa Claus Land Children's Choir. The park advertised it as the world's largest living Christmas tree.

Lewis Sorensen poses with his wax creation of 19th-century actress Lillian Russell. The artist spent several months each year at Santa Claus Land creating new statues and wax figures and maintaining the ones he had already created. His home was in Los Angeles, where he was a stand-in for actor Tyrone Power. Other figures on display were those of Indiana poet James Whitcomb Riley and Abraham Lincoln, who, from age 7 to 21, lived just four miles from what became the town of Santa Claus. Frieda Foertsch, who has worked at the park for 51 years, remembers Sorensen as being "a wonderful guy. He would share all his secrets with me except for his wax formula. I guess he took that to the grave with him."

Wax figures of the Golden Troupe, from New Harmony, Indiana, were featured in the Hall of Famous Americans. Also known as the Golden Family, the famous theatrical group toured the country between the years 1875 and 1890. Wayne Hall, director of food services for the park, remembers working here as a teenager. One of his jobs was to come in late to vacuum the floors of the hall. "We'd get there about 3 a.m., and it was very spooky," he recalls with a laugh. "You'd look up and see Abraham Lincoln there with his ax."

August Mack, a sculptor from Bedford, Indiana, about 90 miles north of Santa Claus Land, created the park's first Santa statue. Mack also created the Mother Goose statue for the park, which still exists above the station at the Freedom Train.

Clowns visiting the park in 1976 converge around the Santa statue.

Bill Koch collected antique cars and by 1958 owned 20 of them. According to an article in *Indiana Business and Industry* published December 1958, he encouraged interest in old cars by sponsoring a race for vintage one-cyclinder automobiles in Santa Claus Land. Entries came from a three-state area to participate in an annual antique car race. Race speeds got up to five miles an hour, according to Jerry Sanders, park archivist.

The German Band, directed by trumpet player Russell Clements from nearby Huntingburg, Indiana, always ended by playing the German national anthem, "The Watch on the Rhine." According to Jim Lammers, who played trombone, the band performed up until Christmas at the outdoor bandstand. "It was very cold," he recalls. "The clarinet players wore gloves without fingers, and we all wore long underwear. But it was fun. We played every Sunday the park was open for about 20 years. Three of us still play with a band we call the Methodist Brass." From left to right are Gerald Reutepohler, Russell Clements, an unidentified musician sitting in for Gordon Werremyer, Jim Lammers, and Donald Bohnenkemper.

54

The Christmas Room was also a place for celebrations. Here on October 29, 1969, three state governors—Illinois's Richard Ogilvy, Indiana's Edgar Whitcomb, and Kentucky's Louie Nunn—dine at the Governors' Dinner in honor of the dedication of the Lincoln Heritage Trail, one of Bill Koch's pet projects. In the far left, in the white uniform, is Romilda Lehr Pund, whose grandchildren now visit the park.

Here is a 1948 menu from the Christmas Room, which seated 240 people. Park president Will Koch remembers a popular option at the end of the meal was Baked Alaska, the flaming ice-cream dessert. "Our family would eat in the Dining Room, later named the Christmas Room, and we would watch a small airplane with a toy Santa figure in it go around in circles as it hung from the ceiling," recalls Will's brother Philip. "I would either have the spaghetti or the cheeseburger, usually the spaghetti. Either way it would be served on Santa Claus Land china. Sometimes Dixie Greulich would be playing the organ, and I would always ask her to play 'Up, Up and Away in My Beautiful Balloon,' if she hadn't already started playing it for me." Full meals are being served again at the Plymouth Rock Café in the Thanksgiving section of the park.

CHRISTMAS DINNERS

ALL DINNERS INCLUDE CHOICE OF

Fruit Cup	Tomato Juice	Grapefruit Juice
	Shrimp Cocktail 25c Extra	
	and	
Onion Soup	Consomme Jellied Consomme	Clam Chowder
	and	
	Vegetable and Potatoes or French Fried Onions	
	and	
Head Lettuce Salad	Combination Salad With French Dressing or Mayonnaise	
	Roquefort Cheese dressing 15c extra	
	and	
Rolls	Coffee or Tea	Ice Cream or Pie

The Blitzen	**$1.65**
FISH STEAK	
Holiday Dinner	**$1.65**
OUR FAMOUS FRIED CHICKEN DINNER	
Star of the East	**$1.95**
HAM STEAK WITH RAISIN SAUCE	
Mrs. Claus Special	**$2.00**
TURKEY DINNER	
The Reindeer	**$1.95**
CHICKEN A LA KING	
Santa's Sleigh	**$1.75**
SWISS STEAK	
The Christmas Tree	**$3.00**
T-BONE STEAK	
Kris Kringle	**$2.50**
FILLET MIGNON	
Fairyland Train	**$1.75**
CHOPPED TENDERLOIN STEAK	
Santa Claus Land Favorite	**$2.25**

The Pre-Christmas Dinner in the Christmas Room in October always drew publicity. According to Jerry Sanders, park archivist, the tradition of the park serving Christmas dinner in the fall began when a reporter named Don Eddy came to Santa Claus Land to write a story for *American Magazine*. Eddy wanted a focal point for his story, and it was decided a good theme was how the staff celebrated Christmas in October as they were too busy in December to do so. This started a tradition for not only the park but also the town of Santa Claus. Featured here is the dessert table. Facing the camera on the left is Violet Tischendorf, who was one of the first employees at Santa Claus Land. Her daughter-in-law Macy Schmitt still works in the park's merchandise department. Schmitt's mother, Laura Stone, was also employed by the park.

The Christmas Room restaurant opened in 1946; this photograph, which dates from that time period, shows the original murals and flooring. According to Will Koch, one of the principal attractions of the park when it first opened was the chicken dinners served there. "My dad told me people lined up for miles down the road for the Sunday lunches they served here." Santa Jim Yellig's wife, Isabelle, was the hostess when the Christmas Room first opened. One of Pat Koch's first jobs at the park after she married Bill was to manage the restaurant. Shortly after assuming her role, she implemented what she thought was a great idea—to outfit the waitresses in elf costumes. "It was not perceived as a good idea," says Pat, laughing about her choice some four decades later. "I can recall one person saying, 'I don't know what Mr. Louie [the founder of Santa Claus Land] would say.'"

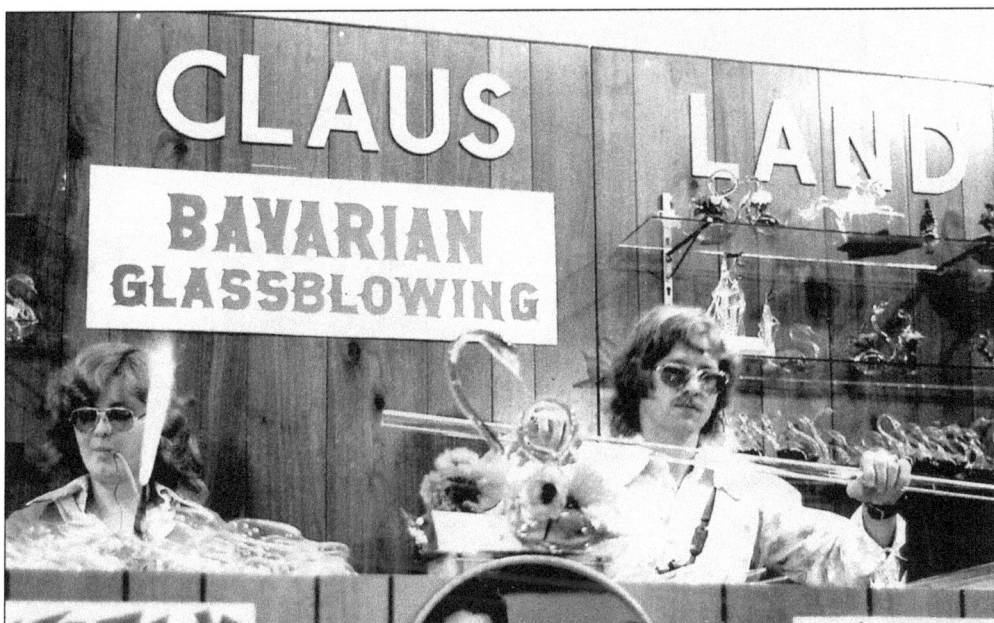

Bavarian glassblowers Kathy and John Warner have worked at the park for decades, creating glass figurines of birds, dogs, horses, ships, and countless other delightful objects. Kathy learned how to blow glass from her father, John Cudequest, who also worked at Santa Claus Land and made the unicorns for the premiere season of *The Glass Menagerie*, a long-running Broadway play.

Music has always been an important part of the park's entertainment. Here is an early-1970s photograph of the Santa Claus Children's Choir, directed by John Schum. Bill and Pat Koch's children Will and Kristi performed in the choir as did Dee Ann Woolems, now the park's director of admissions. "There were children from all over the area," Dee Ann recalls. "It was so much fun."

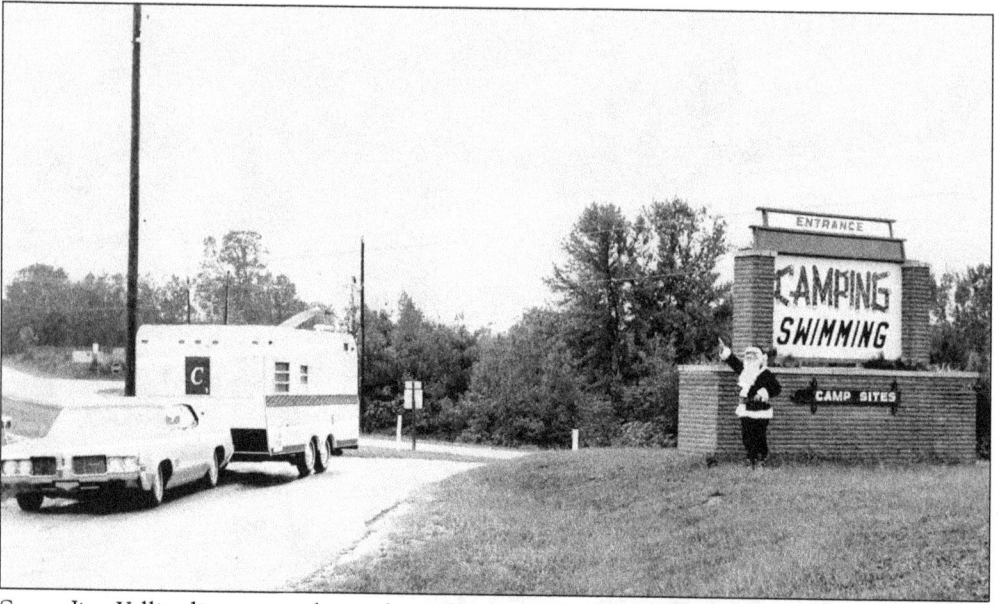

Santa Jim Yellig directs people to the Lake Rudolph Campground. "My father started this campground in 1958 as Lake Rudolph Campsites," says Bill and Pat's youngest son, Philip, president of Ho Ho Holdings LLC. Philip and his sister Kristi Koch George own the campground plus Kringle Place Shopping Center. Philip notes that the campground has had several names over the years, including Holiday World Outdoor Resort and Lake Rudolph Outdoor Resort. It is now called the Lake Rudolph Campground and RV Resort.

"We have grown because the attendance at Holiday World has grown over the years, and I have no doubt that our growth has helped to increase the attendance at Holiday World," says Philip Koch.

Kristi Koch George remembers riding her bike to the beach "every day, every summer" before she started working full time at the park. "We spent the summers on the beach," says Pat Koch. "The kids went down there every morning at 6 a.m. to take swimming lessons."

Kristi Koch George used to ride her horse, Prancer, from the barn behind the family home, past Lake Rudolph, and back around to her horse show. Her little sister, Natalie, used to accompany her, and it is one of Natalie's best memories of the park. The campground has grown to include rental RVs and cabins and a variety of amenities. (Photograph courtesy of Lake Rudolph Campground and RV Resort.)

At one time, it cost 12¢ to enter the House of Dolls. The attraction, now called the Betsy Ross Doll House, boasts more than 2,000 dolls from all over the world and has been part of the park since the late 1940s. Bill Koch's sister Helen Koch Robb assembled the collection and worked at the House of Dolls for many years.

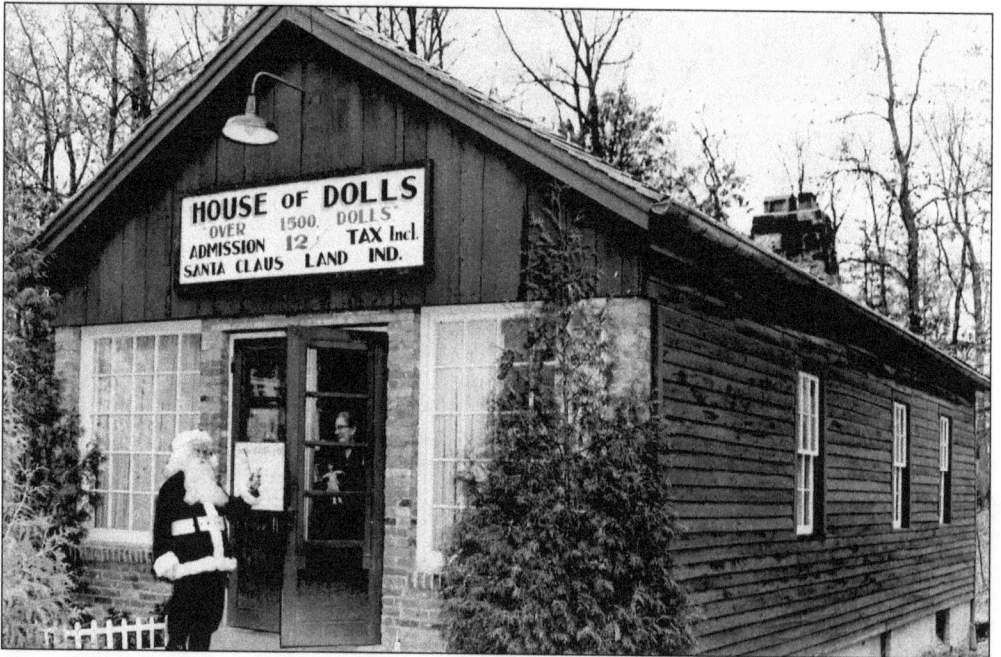

The House of Dolls, which is housed in the original Santa Claus Post Office (it was moved to the park in 1946), is still part of the park's Fourth of July section. Pictured here are Santa Jim Yellig and Frieda Foertsch, who at age 95 still works in the park. Foertsch sewed many of the doll clothes.

Four

ON SANTA'S KNEE

Isabelle Yellig hung Santa's freshly laundered suits on the clothesline at their home. A reporter happened upon this scene and snapped a photograph, which was picked up by the wire service, appearing in newspapers all over the country. Frieda Foertsch, a longtime park employee, used to sew some of Santa Jim Yellig's suits and remembers making two pairs of pants for each outfit. "That way if one of the little children who sat on his lap had an accident, he'd have a pair to change into," she recalls.

More than a million children sat on Santa Jim Yellig's knee over the decades at Santa Claus Land. Young and old were touched by this kindly man with the twinkle in his eye who took his calling to be Santa very seriously. Pat Koch recalls how her dad once delighted a shy child visiting from Germany by speaking in her native language.

Jim Yellig lived in Mariah Hill, a town about four miles from Santa Claus, with his wife, Isabelle, and children Ray and Pat.

As a child, Pat Koch remembers sitting at the dining room table helping her parents answer letters to Santa from children all over the world. Santa Jim answered thousands of letters over the years. This postcard reads, "The most popular person in the park. He is in the park every day to talk to the young and the young at heart."

Natalie Koch did not know that her grandfather was Santa Claus until one day the family settled down in front of the television to watch a news segment featuring Jim Yellig. "That's when I realized he was Santa," she says.

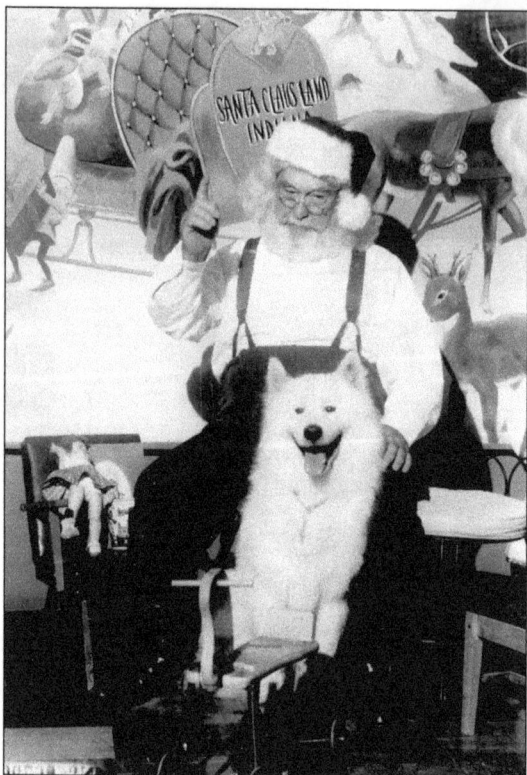

Not only people loved Santa Jim Yellig.
Animals did, too.

Many years after this photograph was taken, Santa Jim's oldest grandson, Will Koch, opened the
Thanksgiving section in Holiday World.

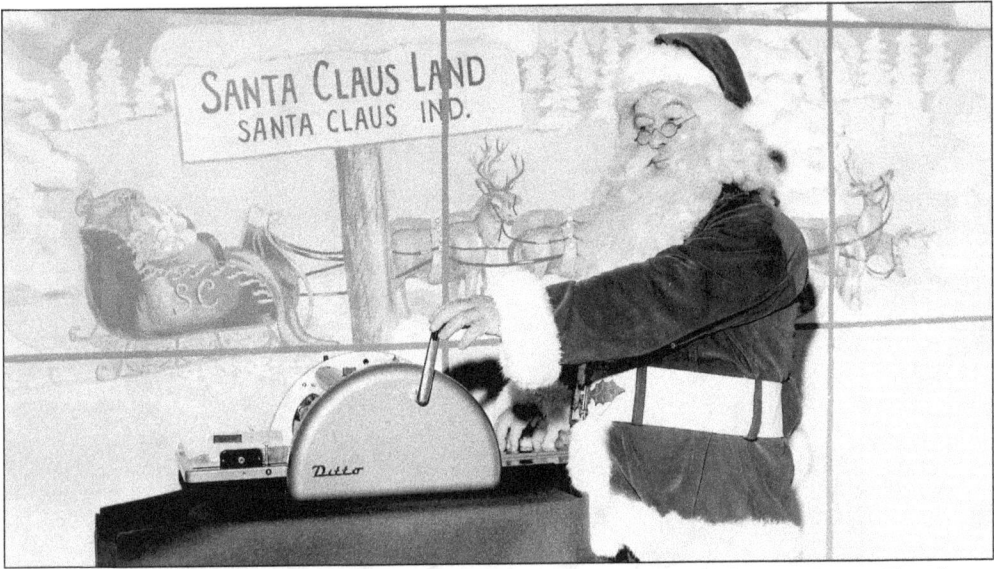

"Jim Yellig was a man who believed in the spirit of Santa Claus and who *was* Santa Claus," says Pat Koch about her father. Santa Jim began his life work as Santa while serving in the navy in 1914 during World War I, where he was stationed in the Brooklyn Navy Yard. The crew held a Christmas party for underprivileged children, and since Jim Yellig liked to talk about coming from a town just outside of Santa Claus, someone suggested him to step in as Santa. After he experienced the joy in children's eyes when they met Santa, Yellig promised that if he survived the war, he would always be Santa.

Santa Jim was a celebrity. Two announcers from WOWO radio traveled from Fort Wayne in northern Indiana to have Santa Jim read *Rudolph the Red-Nosed Reindeer* to them while on the air.

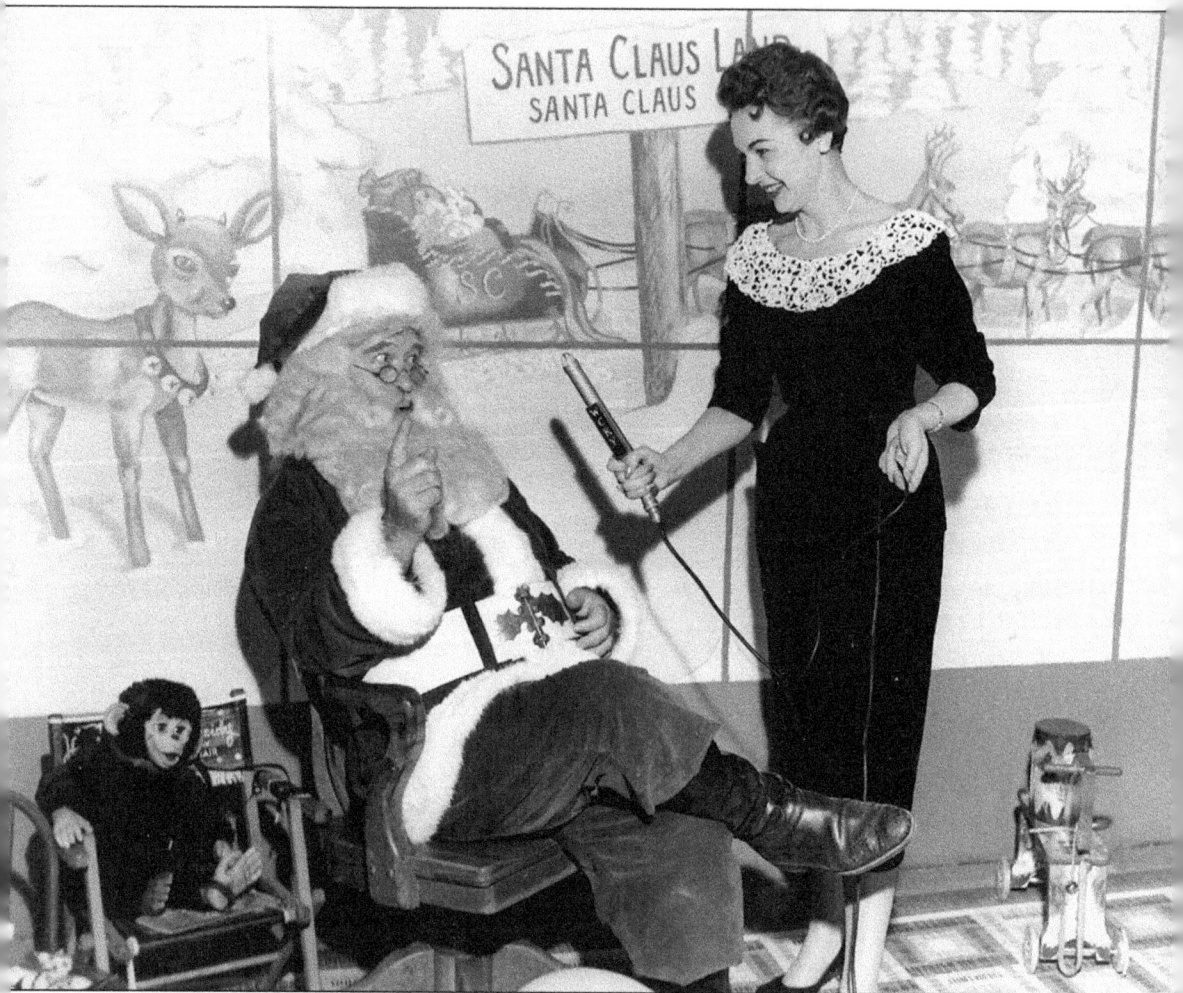

On the air again, Santa Jim Yellig talks to a reporter for WCKY, a Cincinnati radio station. Pat Koch has one of the toys pictured here in her home in Santa Claus.

"A happier, kinder man you couldn't find," says Natalie Koch about her grandfather Santa Jim. "He truly loved children."

The Mesquakie Native American tribe performed in the Pioneer Village at Santa Claus Land in the early 1960s.

Santa Jim Yellig in trouble with the law? More likely it was one of the many publicity shots that he posed for during his years as Santa Claus.

Abraham Lincoln lived in Spencer County, where Santa Claus is located, from the age of 7 to 21. Bill Koch was instrumental in establishing the Lincoln Boyhood National Memorial, which is just four miles down the road from Santa Claus. Here Santa Jim poses with actors portraying the 16th president and his political opponent Stephen Douglas, whom Lincoln debated in 1856 while running for president.

"I found out my grandfather was Santa when I was in first grade," remembers Kristi Koch George. "I found a poster in the basement of him wearing his Santa pants. I think it was an ad for beer, which I know wouldn't be acceptable today but is part of that era." Kristi remembers her grandfather as "absolutely loving children. I don't know how he didn't get tired of having kids sit in his lap or playing Santa, but he didn't. If it was a slow day at the park and there weren't many visitors, he'd entertain the workers. In his Santa suit, not in his Santa suit, he was always Santa." In the background, Isabelle Yellig is seen decorating the family Christmas tree.

"I'm still finding boxes of letters that he kept," says Pat Koch about her father, Santa Jim Yellig, seen here in his later years. Santa Jim was Santa at Santa Claus Land for nearly four decades. According to Pat, he wrote notes on the letters he received from children so he could personalize each reply.

Santa read a Christmas story over the air to Fort Wayne–area children thanks to WOWO radio. When people ask Pat Koch how long her father played Santa, she responds, "Never. He didn't *play* Santa Claus, he *was* Santa Claus." Koch still treasures her father's original Santa suit, buckles, and boots.

Santa greeted people from all over the world.

You are never too old to sit on Santa's lap, no matter what your age! When this photograph was taken, J. D. Bockstahler, a longtime resident of Santa Claus and the man sitting on Santa Jim's knee, was in his 90s.

Both Santa Jim Yellig and his son, Ray, had long and distinguished careers in the navy.

Santa Jim poses with Miss Indiana in 1963. "I always remember being at my grandfather's house on Christmas Eve," recalls Philip Koch. "Throughout the evening, he would get numerous telephone calls. He would answer these calls and talk in a different voice and shake his sleigh bells. I feel really stupid now, but I never made the connection that he was actually Santa."

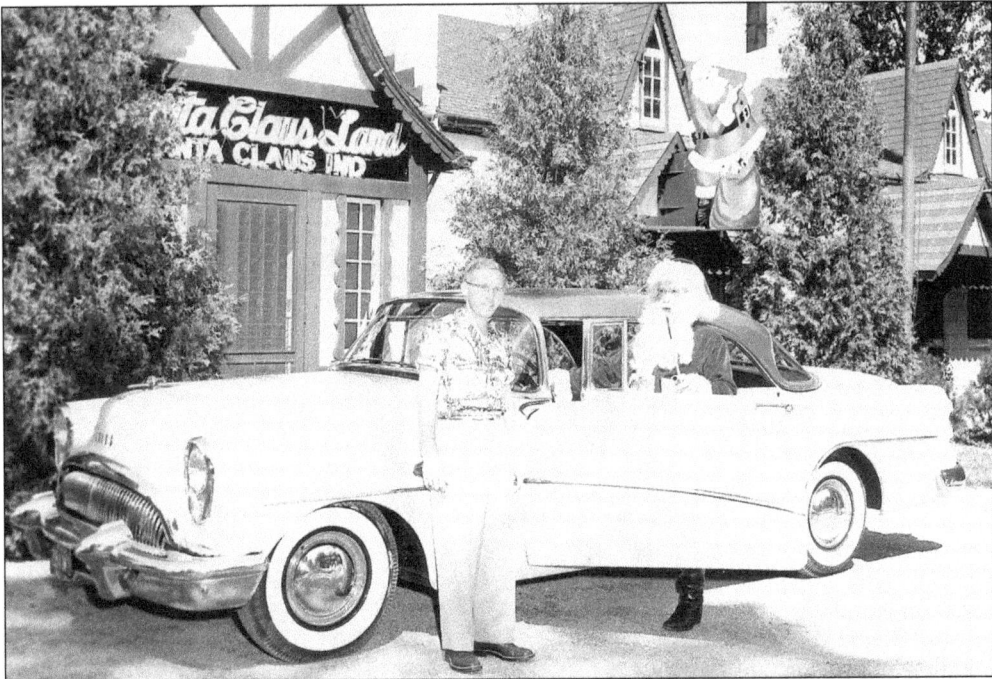

When Santa Jim rode in parades, Pat Koch would often ride along with him and help him toss candy along the parade route. Here is Santa Jim with one of his favorite cars, which was white with a red top.

Santa Jim Yellig is pictured with Bill Koch and a fellow legionnaire.

"My grandfather was a vivacious fellow who really loved his grandkids," recalls Bill and Pat Koch's middle son, Dan, of Santa Jim. "He would make up the greatest stories and leave us all spellbound."

"I remember when my Grandmother Yellig and I would make Christmas cookies," recalls Natalie Koch. "My grandmother was a strong German woman who didn't believe in eating the cookies until it was time. My grandfather would stand at the kitchen door and wink at me, and we would try to sneak a cookie. If my grandmother caught us, she would good-naturedly scold us."

Santa Jim, at home in Mariah Hill, kept busy with yard work amidst his year-round Christmas decorations. His grandson Will now has the Santa and reindeer statues in his yard.

Santa Jim Yellig passed away at age 90 in 1984 just as Santa Claus Land was becoming Holiday World. Generations of children will always remember him.

Five

GENERATIONS

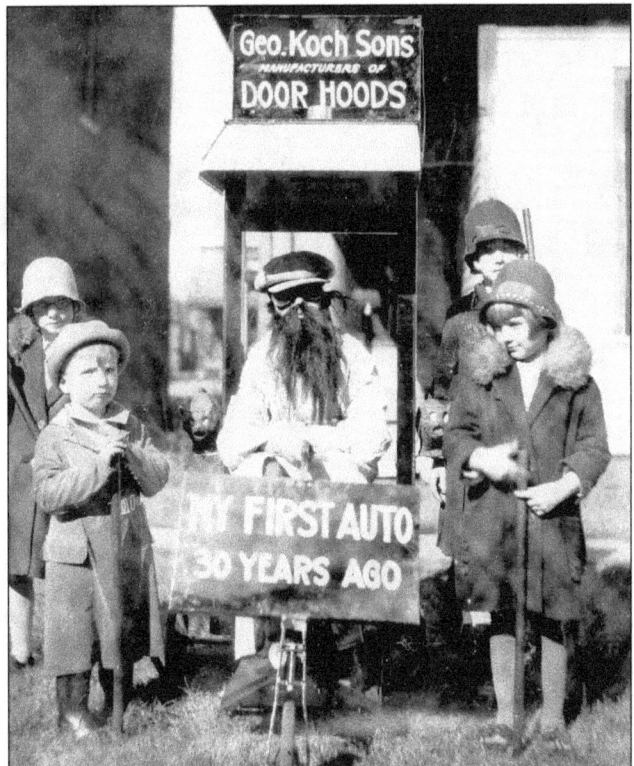

Bill Koch, in a beard, hat, and goggles, was five years old when this parade photograph was taken. Several of his siblings are included in this 1920 photograph in Evansville.

In 1873, George Koch started working in the tin business in Evansville, Indiana. He founded George Koch Sons, which still exists as part of Koch Enterprises. George had three sons—Louis J., Albert, and George W.—who were active in the family business. Louis J. Koch went on to found Santa Claus Land in 1946.

This 1950s family photograph shows the Louis J. and Clarice Koch family at their 50th wedding anniversary. In early years, almost every family member played a part in Santa Claus Land's development and success. From left to right are (first row) Mary Helen Robb, Louis J., Clarice, and Virginia Cavanaugh; (second row) Ashburn Koch, Martha Lois Long, Robert Koch, Malcolm Koch, L. J. Koch III, Katheryne Bosse, and Bill Koch.

A 1937 Purdue graduate, Bill Koch completed postgraduate work in naval architecture at the U.S. Naval Academy in Annapolis, Maryland. He served in the navy in World War II, helping to coordinate the repair of damaged ships at Pearl Harbor, including the USS *Indiana*. At first, Koch was somewhat hesitant about joining his father in the Santa Claus Land project but then saw the potential for this small-town theme park, the first in the world. Koch was a man of vision, and in his lifetime would build Santa Claus Land into a well-known and loved attraction.

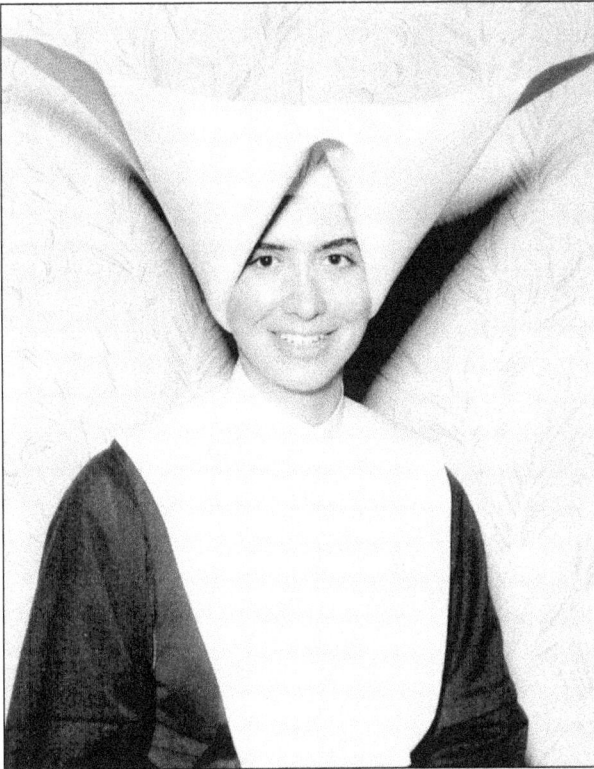

Pat Yellig graduated from high school at age 16. She graduated as a registered nurse from Hotel Dieu Sisters' Hospital in New Orleans and received a bachelor of science degree in nursing from St. Louis University in Missouri. Yellig belonged to the Daughters of Charity of St. Vincent DePaul for 10 years.

Bill and Pat Koch began their 40-year marriage on December 27, 1960. "I used to tease him, 'You may be older, but I'm smarter,'" remembers Pat of their 16-year age difference. On the left of the newlyweds is Pat's mother, Isabelle; the groom shakes hands with his father-in-law, Santa Jim Yellig. The German Band, which performed at the park for 20 years, played at the wedding. Pat donated the dress her mother wore in this photograph to the local high school, and it was worn in a play in 2005.

In this 1963 photograph, Pat Koch holds nine-month-old Kristi on her lap, two-year-old Will reaches for a drum, and Bill hands his baby daughter one of the many toys in the park's Toy Shop. Pat and Bill had five children in six years. After the birth of their fifth child, Natalie, Bill gave Pat five dozen roses with a card that read, "Five dozen red roses for your 5th child. One dozen for each. But I can't afford six dozen. Love, Bill."

Santa Jim is surrounded by four of his grandchildren. Clockwise from top are Will, Dan, Philip, and Kristi Koch, with their mother, Pat.

Being the children of a theme park owner certainly had its perks, but one of them certainly was not having to dress in itchy costumes on summer days. "It was very hot wearing those costumes," says Will Koch, now president of Holiday World and Splashin' Safari. Koch's first job, which he started at the age of 10, was to walk around the park in an elf costume. On the right is Kristi Koch, now a neurologist in Indianapolis, but a reindeer at age nine.

Santa Jim Yellig prepares to pose for publicity photographs with his daughter, Pat Koch, and Philip and Natalie, Pat and Bill's two youngest children.

Will Koch, now president of Holiday World and Splashin' Safari, remembers going to the airport with his father to pick up costumes, which had been flown in from New York. "Dad made me put the costume on in the car so that I could show everybody what it looked like when we got to the park," recalls Koch. Happy Kellems the clown stands behind Santa Jim. Koch, dressed as an elf, is on the left, next to Patty Braun, while Dan Koch, another elf, is on the right in between Becky Ringeman (standing) and Denise Mullis.

Happy Kellems is seen with Kristi and two of her three brothers, who are dressed as elves.

Family time was very important to the Koch family. Pat Koch remembers that when they went out to dinner, her three boys usually wore suits, and the two girls wore dresses and patent leather shoes. And they were always expected to be on their best behavior. From left to right are Bill, Will, Philip, Pat, Natalie, Dan, and Kristi.

The Koch children are seen around the Santa statue in a photograph taken for the family's 1969 Christmas card. From left to right are Will, Dan, Philip, Kristi, and Natalie.

Two years later, the family poses for this photograph with Fr. Joseph Ziliak, a friend of the family. From left to right are Kristi, Pat holding Natalie, Dan, Will, and Philip in front of his father, Bill.

The Koch family traveled to Washington, D.C., for a family vacation. Here they stand in front of the Capitol with Congressman Roger Zion of Indiana's Eighth District. From left to right are Pat, Kristi, Natalie, Philip, Dan, and Will. The two men behind the children are Congressman Zion on the left and Bill Koch on the right.

This 1973 photograph shows the Koch family on vacation in Gatlinburg, Tennessee. "We would visit theme parks with our parents when we went on vacation," recalls the youngest Koch child, Natalie. "Dad had a dual purpose for going. We'd be the guinea pigs, and he would see what we liked about the park and what we didn't. Gatlinburg has a lot of souvenirs, and Dad would want to look at them, too. He was a phenomenal businessman, and he was a phenomenal father. We always knew that he really loved and wanted to be with us." From left to right are Dan, Philip, Natalie, Kristi, Will, and cousin Kathy Long with Pat and Bill.

Pat Koch (center back) still remembers this dress and hat. To the left of Pat is family friend Mary Virginia Clark and on her right, Pat's mother, Isabelle Yellig, her husband, Jim, and their son, Ray. Bill Koch is on the left and the children from left to right are Dan, Will, Kristi, Natalie, and Philip. The photograph was taken at St. Joseph Church in Dale on Will's first communion day.

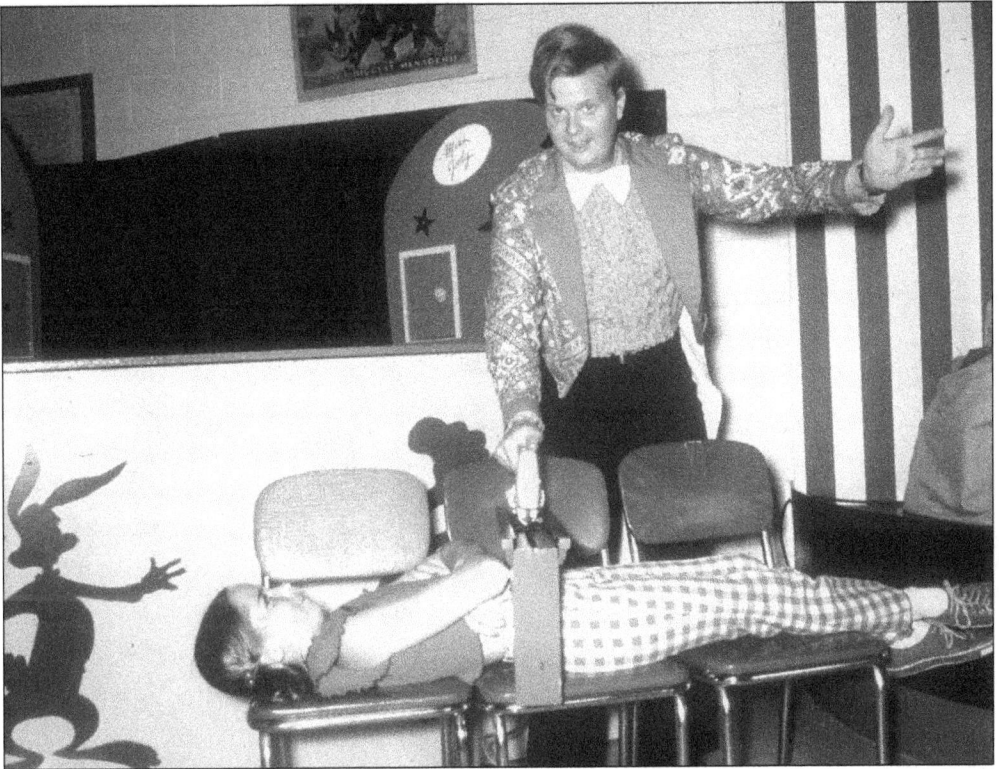

Magician Art Bausman prepares to saw Kristi Koch in half. With these types of childhood experiences, is it any wonder she became a doctor?

Kristi Koch is pictured here with Miss Judy, one of the Educated Animals. Here Miss Judy ponders under which cup an object is hidden.

The Koch siblings, all grown up, sit at the kitchen table with their father, Bill Koch, in 1989. From left to right are Bill, Kristi, Philip, Will, Natalie, and Dan.

Lori Morris from Onward, Indiana, met her future husband while performing at Santa Claus Land. Lori married Will Koch in 1985. Their children, though still in school, also work at the park. Dave Girton, owner of Encore International, produces the shows at the park. He remembers Will and Lori meeting at one of his shows. "I was in their wedding, and now their daughter Lauren is in our shows." Girton says what the Kochs have done with the park "is founded on great qualities and because of that they have a faithful following."

Like mother like daughter. Lauren Koch, Will and Lori's older daughter, performs at Holiday World.

One of Will Koch's hobbies was taking photographs.

Leah Koch, Will and Lori's younger daughter, works at the park during the summer. This photograph was taken by her father for use in a German magazine in late 2004. Leah wrote an article for the magazine. Here is an excerpt: "I am fourteen years old and I am in the eighth grade. When I'm not busy with school, I like to dance, play my bass guitar, practice my oboe, and play piano. I live in a town called Santa Claus in Indiana. My family runs a theme park called Holiday World and my grandmother leads an organization called Santa's Elves but more about that later. The town, of course, gets many letters to Santa Claus and someone has to answer them. Santa's Elves come in to help with that. Formed in 1974, it is a non-profit organization that answers those letters. My grandmother, being an 'elf' has helped keep up with the 10,000 letters they receive every year. All in all, Santa Claus is a fun place to live, from Holiday World to the elaborate Christmas celebrations. There are so many things to do; it's like celebrating Christmas all year long. Before I leave, I would like to wish you a very Merry Christmas."

Will Koch with his wife, Lori, and three children are seen here. From left to right are (first row) Leah and Lauren; (second row) William Koch III. This photograph was taken in 1996, the year after the Raven opened. Of course, it was a posed portrait, and the family did not ride the coaster together in this manner. William was, in fact, too small to ride the Raven until a number of years after this photograph was taken. (Photograph courtesy of Erik Photographic.)

Natalie Koch was the first director of Splashin' Safari. After earning a master's degree in Latin American studies, Koch returned to the park to help with the 1993 start-up of the new water park. In 2000, she was interviewed about her work and told writer Michael Nolan for an article in *American Profile* that working at the family park was "rewarding. I see how employees benefit from working here and grow and improve. It sounds kind of corny but they do become part of our family." The 1996 photograph includes, from left to right, Natalie, Angie Uebelhor, and Andy Hildenbrand.

Isabelle Yellig is surrounded by a granddaughter and multiple great-grandchildren. From left to right are Lauren Koch (Will's daughter) holding Alexa (Philip's daughter, who was born on Christmas Day), Will's other daughter Leah holding Kristi's younger son Adam George, Isabelle holding William A. Koch III, Kristi's older son Nicholas George, and youngest grandchild Natalie holding Philip's son, Logan.

Santa Jim Yellig fell off the roof and broke his leg while shoveling snow from the roof of his family restaurant, the Chateau. When people at the hospital recognized Santa Claus, they asked him to pose for a photograph, which appeared in the newspaper.

Will Koch's first big project for Holiday World was Raging Rapids. Here he, Santa, and Bill Koch break ground for the ride in 1989. Will, a roller coaster aficionado who has an electrical engineering degree from Notre Dame, participates in the creation and design of the roller coasters at the park.

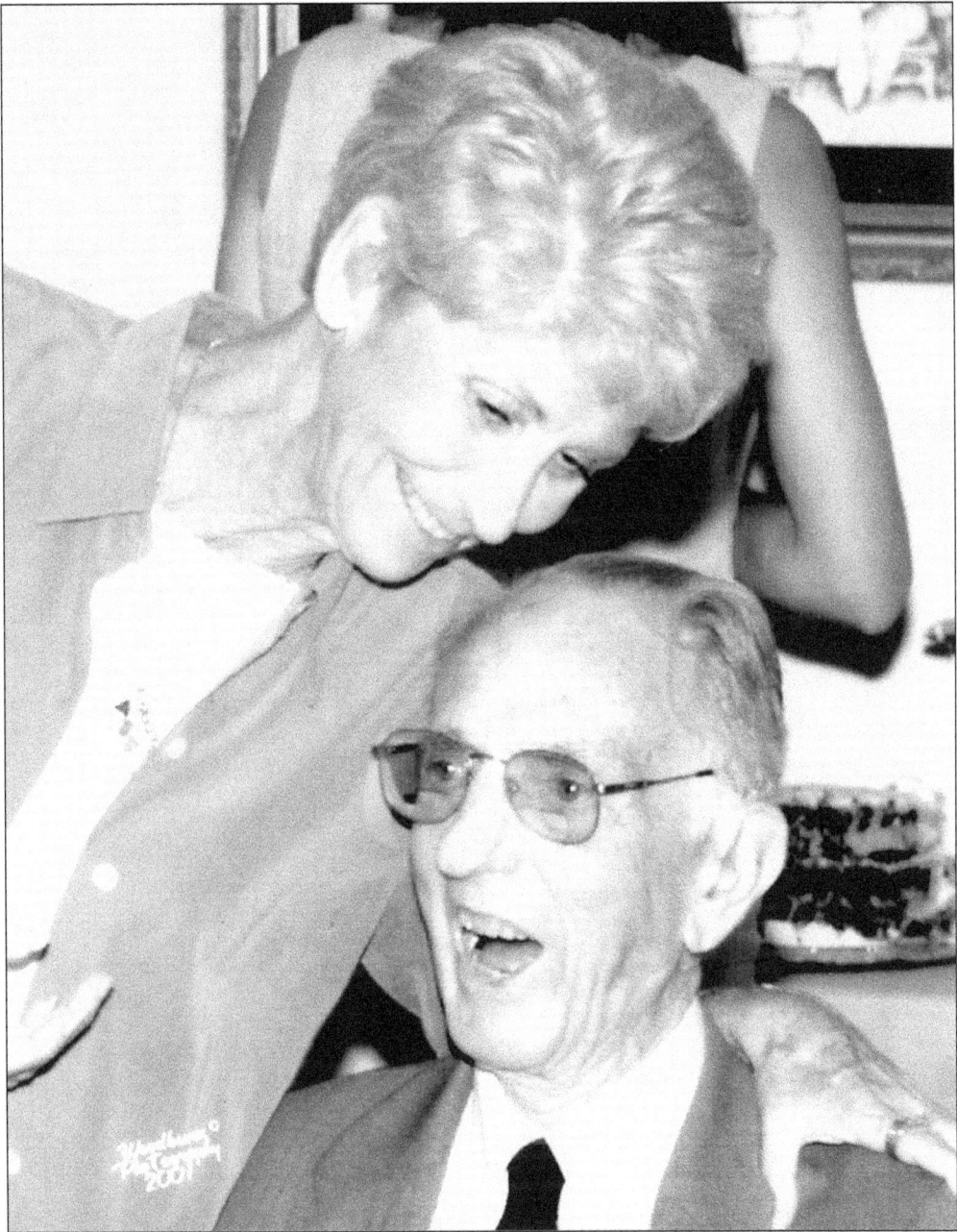

This is one of the last photographs of Bill and Pat Koch, taken a month before Bill's death on September 17, 2001, at age 86. At his father's funeral, Will Koch said, "I remember as a young boy seeing in Dad's office at what was then Santa Claus Land a quote from Robert Kennedy: 'Some men see things as they are and say why? I dream things that never were and say why not?' This quotation captures the essence of Dad's philosophy of life." Bill Koch's imprint on Santa Claus and on southern Indiana reflects his dynamism. This photograph was taken during Pat's 70th birthday party.

This Koch family photograph was taken in 2004. From left to right are (first row) Natalie's husband Eric King, Natalie holding Anna King, Pat Koch, Dan holding daughter Erin, and Dan's wife Kristin holding David William Koch; (second row) Nicholas George and William Koch III; (third row) Philip's fiancée Carol Ruch, Philip's daughter Alexa, Philip and his son Logan, Kristi Koch George with her children Marie and Adam and husband Jim George, and Will and Lori Koch with their daughters Lauren and Leah. Not pictured is Mary King, born in July 2005. The Koch family holds a reunion every year around the time of the birthday of Louis J. Koch, the founder of Santa Claus Land.

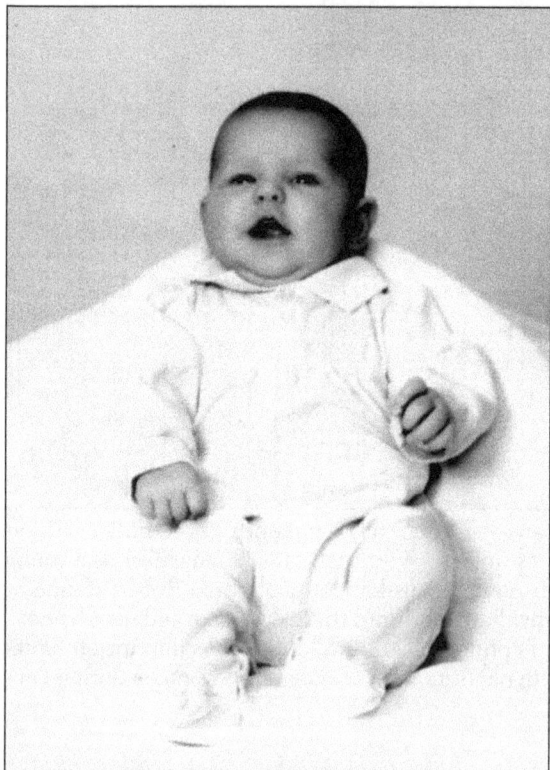

Mary King, the newest addition to the Koch family, is seen here in 2005.

Six

HOLIDAY WORLD AND SPLASHIN' SAFARI

Santa Claus Land became Holiday World in 1984, with the addition of themed Halloween and Fourth of July sections. Bill and Pat Koch pose in front of the park's Santa statue, located in the first holiday-themed section guests experience when they enter the park, Christmas.

Frightful Falls log flume was added the year Santa Claus Land became Holiday World. William Koch III continues the family tradition of posing for publicity photographs while riding with cousins Nicholas George, Logan Koch, and William's sister Leah.

A news release issued prior to the start of the 1993 season promised that the new Splashin' Safari would continue to grow for five years, with a total budget of $3 million. More than a decade later, Indiana's largest water park continues to grow in size and popularity.

Thunder Bumpers on Chesapeake Bay were added to the park in 1977; they are still a popular ride.

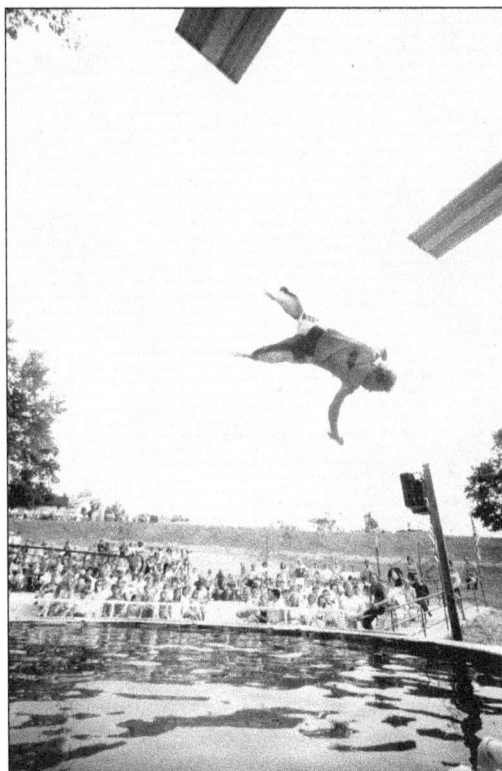

Holiday World and Splashin' Safari's live entertainment includes a rollicking high-dive show, which ranges from comedic antics to Olympic-style diving. Notice the background of this photograph; it was taken before 1995, when the Raven was built.

Frieda Foertsch was named Indiana's Outstanding Older Worker in 2000, winning a trip to Washington, D.C., and a visit with Indiana's congressional delegation. Foertsch, who was born in 1910, began working at the park in 1954. She still works at the park, and her duties include supervising the planting of 3,000 annuals each spring.

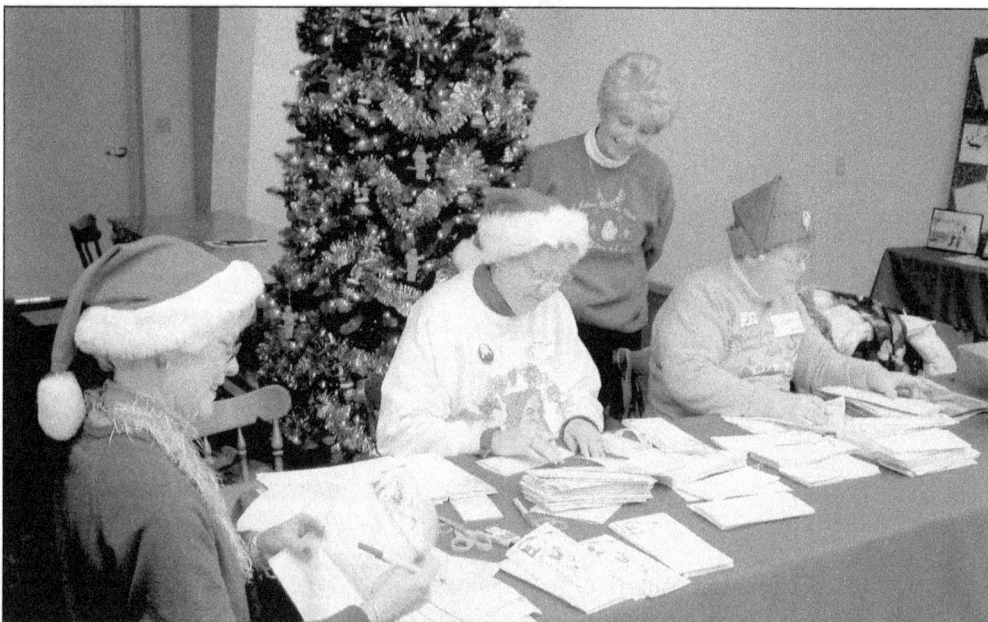

Members of the Christmas Lake Village Garden Club gather to answer letters to Santa. Seated, from left to right, are Judy Carrell, Faye Rupprecht, and Joyce Robinson; Pat Koch is standing. The Santa's Elves Inc. became a nonprofit organization in 1974, with postmaster Mary Ann Long on the first board of directors. Its purpose is to continue the century-long tradition of answering letters to Santa.

100

Holidog and his pals George the Eagle and Safari Sam greet children of all ages with waves and hugs.

Holidog has his own roller coaster. It is part of Holidog's FunTown, which Will Koch designed in 1999 to give younger guests and their families a fun place to ride, climb, and play.

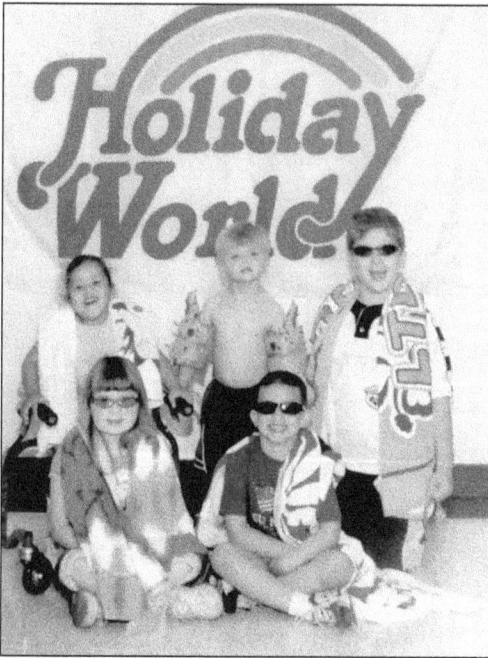

"Each spring on Play Day, we open the park for the invited guests of the Easter Seals Rehabilitation Center," says Holiday World president Will Koch. "At Holiday World, we strive to be a park where children and adults with physical and mental disabilities can feel comfortable and safe, and have a really fun time. On Play Day, we open our gates to some very special guests—and see some of the happiest smiles of the season." Holiday World's Play Day has raised more than $135,000 for the Easter Seals Rehabilitation Center in Evansville, Indiana.

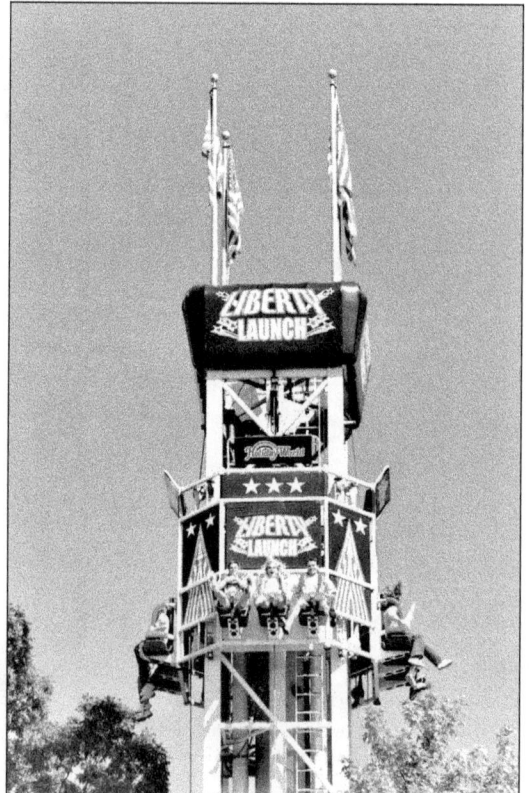

Added to Holiday World's Fourth of July section in 2003, Liberty Launch gives patriots a double thrill.

"I remember the reaction we received when we won the International Applause Award at the 2004 IAAPA Convention," says John Chidester. The park's director of marketing remembers that day in Orlando, Florida, during the International Association of Amusement Parks and Attractions (IAAPA) convention: "It certainly was one of my best days on the job. I was sitting in the row directly behind the Koch family. After they announced the three finalists, the ballroom was filled with anticipation yet eerily quiet. As they began to announce our name, we all heard the word 'Holiday,' but no one heard 'World' because of the spontaneous roar of applause from the audience. Will sat in his chair motionless for a moment as Mrs. Koch leapt into the air screaming at the top of her lungs. She then turned and gave me a huge hug as she continued screaming wildly in my ear as I twirled her round and round in the aisle. Soon we were mobbed in the aisle by friends from parks located all around the world." From left to right are Mats Wedin, CEO of Liseberg Park, cosponsor of the award with *Amusement Business* magazine; Will Koch; Pat Koch; and Dan Koch. (Photograph courtesy Amusement Business magazine.)

In 2002, returning seasonal hosts and hostesses were treated to a special presentation by *Survivor* contestant Rodger "Kentucky Joe" Bingham, who talked about the importance of "giving your all" in every aspect of life. One of the final "survivors" in the Australian Outback series, Bingham is shown here with seasonal park employee John Kenworthy, who spoke to his peers about his experience as a cancer survivor. A popular ride operator, Kenworthy was planning to return for another season when he passed away in the spring of 2003; he was just 26 years old.

Many parents come off the Lewis and Clark Trail, added in 1978, teasing their young children about their driving skills.

The Howler is the perfect ride for young roller coaster enthusiasts.

After the huge success of the free unlimited soft drinks (sampled in this photograph by Molly Chidester, the younger daughter of the park's director of marketing), which was launched in 2000, Will Koch invited his staff of directors to dream up some other over-the-top customer service ideas. Splashin' Safari's Lori Gogel suggested free sunscreen, which was added in 2002. Also on the list of park freebies are free parking and free use of inner tubes in Splashin' Safari. The park is also smoke-free.

Pat Koch pauses near ZOOMbabwe, the world's largest enclosed waterslide. She is affectionately called the Queen of Clean because of her determination to keep the park spotless; she is often seen cleaning in the park. Though now in her 70s, she continues to work a full schedule, never slowing down. "I hope I can be like my mom when I'm her age," says her daughter Kristi Koch George.

The Congo River was part of Splashin' Safari when it opened in 1993. It is so popular that a second action river, Bahari River, was added in 2006.

From the top of ZOOMbabwe, acres of Splashin' Safari stretch out in all directions. Park president and general manager Will Koch often tells reporters, "Adding Splashin' Safari was the best business decision we ever made." *Zinga*, the Swahili word for "to move in a circular motion" offers families a wild water ride they can enjoy together. Zinga was voted the world's second-best water park ride by the readers of *Amusement Today* magazine in 2005.

Bahari is the Swahili word for "immense sea." Splashin' Safari's second wave pool lives up to the word! The themed rock work, including carved tiki fountains, adds an exotic atmosphere.

Pat Koch helps out the ride operators at HallowSwings. One of the reasons Holiday World and Splashin' Safari have been so successful is that the Koch family believes in being out in their parks, setting a good example. "I can't tell you how many guests have e-mailed us later, astounded that 'the woman on the commercials' was actually at the park," says Paula Werne, director of public relations. "In the morning, she greets families outside the front gate, welcoming them. Later in the day, she works her way through the parks, helping where she's needed. She may be at a ride, a game, slicing pizza in a restaurant, or checking to be sure the walkways and restrooms are free of trash."

"When our graphic artist and marketing staff were designing the artwork for HallowSwings back in the fall of 2002, Mrs. Koch was concerned about whether the Halloween icons would be 'scary Halloween' or 'fun Halloween,'" recalls Paula Werne. "She needn't have worried, even the skulls are smiling."

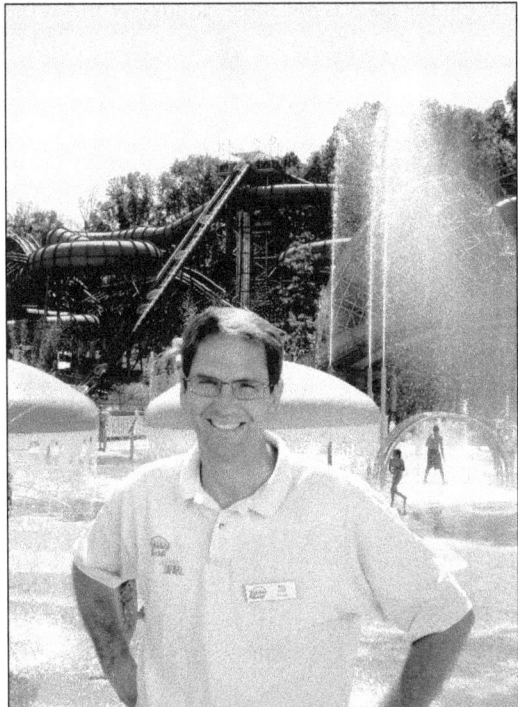

Will Koch added Jungle Jets to Splashin' Safari in 2004; the huge "sprayground" includes more than 160 water-play elements.

Raging Rapids was added to Holiday World's Fourth of July section in 1990.

Seven

WOOD IS GOOD

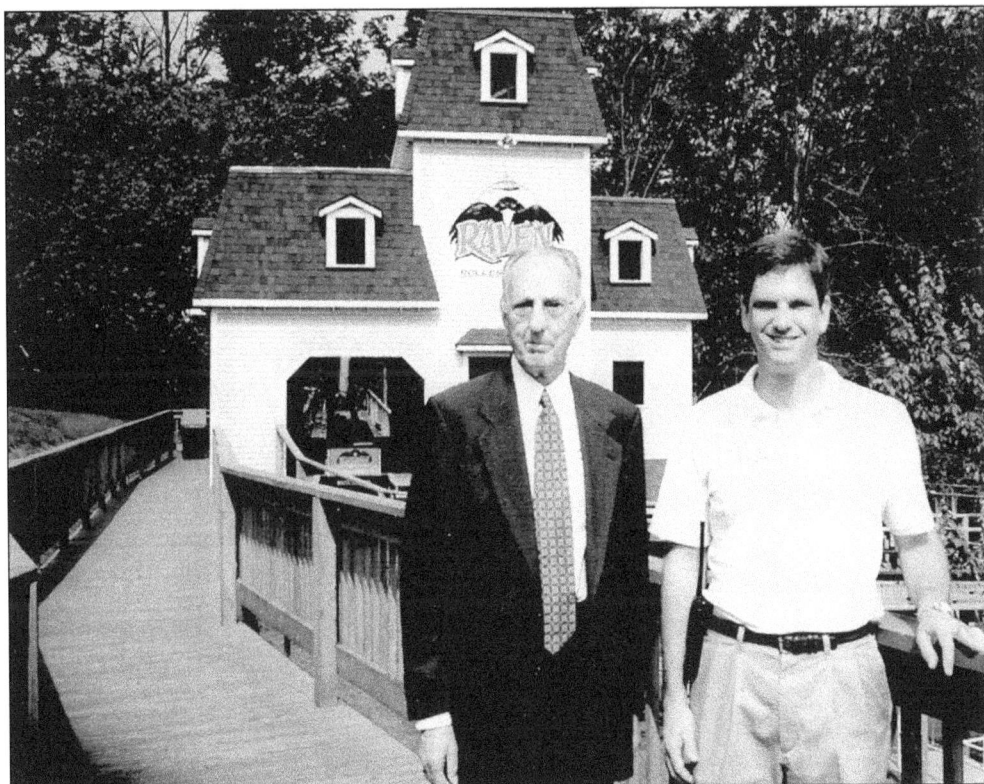

Bill and Will Koch stand in front of the Raven, at that time the largest wooden roller coaster in Indiana and Kentucky. (That record was broken in 2000 when The Legend opened and again in 2006 with the premiere of the Voyage, both also Holiday World coasters.) "The Raven was the realization of a dream Dad and I shared for years," says Will. "My recollection is we talked about it a lot; we believed that adding a big coaster would put us on the map. And we were right!"

Construction of the Raven began in 1994. This banked curve swoops over Lake Rudolph.

The Raven, which opened in 1995, was repeatedly voted the world's number one wooden roller coaster by the readers of *Amusement Today*. More than a decade after opening, it continues to rank among the top-five wooden coasters on the planet.

Lt. Gov. Frank O'Bannon and Will Koch ride the Raven in May 1995 in celebration of National Tourism Week. Seated behind them are state representative Sally Rideout Lambert and Indiana director of tourism John Goss. Holiday World hosted a luncheon that day for regional tourism professionals, and Koch invited his guests to ride the Raven. One of the sisters from the Monastery Immaculate Conception in nearby Ferdinand later told the story that someone remarked, "Oh, you must have prayed the entire time you were on that ride." Sister Sylvia, who was in her 70s, responded with a wink, "Oh, I knew even God couldn't help me!"

Santa Claus was all grins after riding the Raven with Natalie Koch on the "first flight" during the preopening Media Preview. Santa later commented that riding the Raven was the closest experience he had ever had to that annual sleigh ride he takes each Christmas Eve. Later that season, a writer with the *Chicago Sun-Times* newspaper wrote, "Santa's beard was probably black before he rode The Raven."

Bill Koch, the man who turned a small-town theme park into one of the most beloved parks in the country, cuts the ribbon in the opening ceremony for the Raven. His granddaughter Leah Koch opted at the last minute not to ride that first ride. "We left that seat open," remembers the park's public relations director, Paula Werne. "I didn't want to delay the ceremony, so I called out, 'Let's leave it for the ghost of Edgar Allan Poe!' and everyone laughed."

Will Koch cheers, along with the other riders, as the Raven, the park's first wooden roller coaster, returns to the station. This was the very first test ride on the Raven. Next to Koch is Steve Meunier, director of development, who has worked at the park for 20 years. Before park employees were allowed to ride, sacks of corn were loaded into the trains to add the appropriate weight to help keep the train moving around the track. Several of the bags burst during those early rides, and later in the summer, stalks of corn were found growing out in the woods under the track of the Raven.

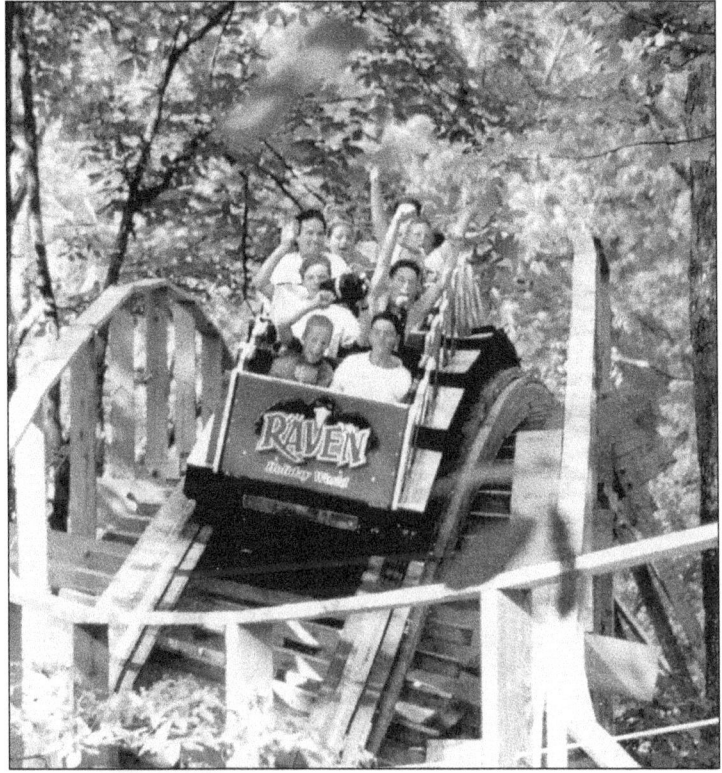

Forbes American Heritage magazine named the Raven a "Top Ten Roller Coaster" with the following commentary: "The Raven was responsible for a sudden turn in roller-coaster design. The park and the coaster designer got the idea to forgo bragging rights for height and speed in favor of focusing on the quality of the ride. The result . . . blew everyone away."

Nia Ammeson rides the Raven with Will Koch. It is a photograph the girl still treasures, five years after it was taken, and exemplifies the park's friendliness and family focus. When the girl's mother, one of the authors of this book, was too timid to ride the coaster, Koch stepped in to help out. Ammeson was delighted to discover that she and Koch share the same birthday.

Members of the American Coaster Enthusiasts (ACE) pose for a group photograph in front of the Raven. About 300 ACEers attended their Spring Conference at Holiday World on May 19, 1995. Also along was a crew from the CBS news program *48 Hours*, which was filming an episode about thrill seekers.

CBS's *48 Hours* correspondent Richard Schlessenger interviews Lucy White of Florida, the oldest ACE member in attendance at their 1995 Spring Conference, hosted by the park. Holiday World and the Kochs have shared a warm relationship with ACE over the years.

Mick Foley, a wrestling-world icon, loves roller coasters and parks. He invited two Make a Wish children, named Tommy and David (shown here), to spend the day with him at the park in 2002. "Mick was so kind and gentle with the boys throughout the day," recalls Paula Werne, director of public relations for Holiday World. "I may not be a wrestling fan, but I'm a big Mick Foley fan."

All of the park's hosts and hostesses pose in front of the Raven in April 1995 during a pretraining orientation session. Because the park's staff has grown so much in size, orientation now has to be conducted multiple times to include everyone. Brandon Berg, director of human resources for the park, explains how much Pat Koch has meant to him over the years: "She has been an inspiration to me, and I often have called her my second mom. In 1992, I asked her if I could leave a little early so I could make it to the local college to register. I told her it was the deadline and that I was $200 short of the tuition, but all I had to do was find my mom to see if she could loan me the money until I got paid the next day. A couple hours later, Mrs. Koch walked up with a white envelope, and in it was $200. She told me that she was loaning me this money for my tuition. I was just amazed! She had always been an inspiration to me, and that one single act had again proved to me what a truly wonderful and caring person she was. Fast forward to 2006—she's still the same as she was back then, and she's still an inspiration after all this time."

"We held a contest in 1995 and chose 12 couples to be married on the Raven," recalls Paula Werne, director of public relations for the park. "The ceremony was performed by 'Elvis.' His name is Bruce Borders, and at that time, he was the mayor of Jasonville, Indiana. Mayors, of course, can marry couples. He serenaded the couples with, 'Can't Help Falling in Love.' Bruce is now a member of our state legislature."

This photograph shows a few of the couples on the "Roller Coaster of Love." "After we got knee-deep into this project, I remember awakening one morning, paralyzed with fear," recalls Paula Werne. "Working with 12 engaged couples didn't scare me one bit. But then it came to me: 12 mothers-of-the-brides. Happily, all the couples and their families were wonderful—no problems at all. We even received a touching letter a few weeks later from the father of one of the brides, thanking us for treating the wedding ceremony with such respect."

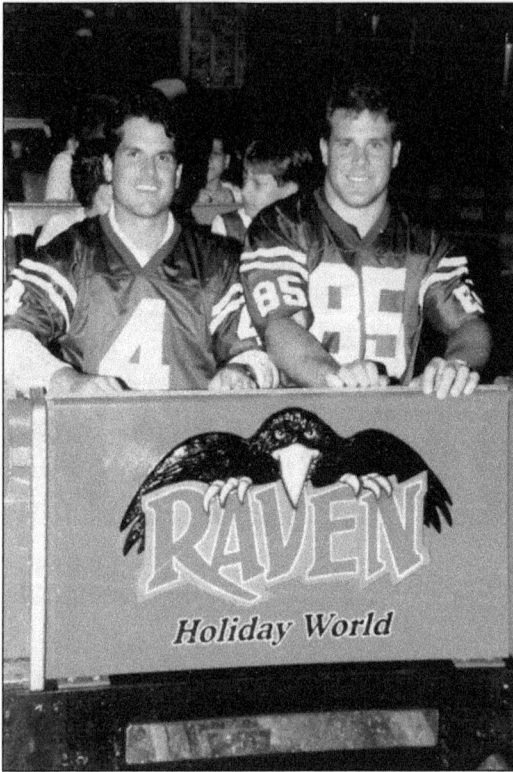

Indianapolis Colts football players Jim Harbaugh (left) and Ken Dilger ride the Raven. Just like Pat Koch, Ken Dilger is a native of nearby Mariah Hill.

The theme of Holiday World's second wooden roller coaster is *The Legend of Sleepy Hollow*, a mid-19th century novel by Washington Irving that featured a headless horseman. Indeed, riders on The Legend race wildly through the woods as if chased by the relentless Headless Horseman. The Legend was the top-ranked new wooden roller coaster for 2000 and continues to be voted a top-10 wooden coaster annually by the readers of *Amusement Today* magazine.

It is tradition to hoist an American flag on top of the highest point of a coaster while it is under construction. Holiday World also added a Christmas tree to The Legend, which opened in 2000.

The Legend wooden roller coaster has several dramatic drops measuring 113 feet, 77 feet, and 64 feet. When Will Koch could not get a helix to "fit" into the layout of his first coaster, the Raven, he was determined to get one into The Legend, and he succeeded.

Bill and Pat Koch "ride" The Legend at the International Association of Amusement Parks and Attractions convention in November 1999.

After 22 years of celebrating Halloween, the Fourth of July, and Christmas, Holiday World added a new holiday-themed section in 2006. The Thanksgiving section opened with the Voyage wooden roller coaster and Gobbler Getaway, an interactive dark ride.

The Voyage features three drops of over 100 feet with the first drop's angle of descent is a steep 66 degrees. The top speed of the three-train coaster is 67.4 miles per hour. "The Voyage is an air-time machine with riders experiencing a feeling of weightlessness for a total of 24.2 seconds," says Will Koch, who helped create and design the roller coaster, which was introduced in 2006 as part of the park's 60th anniversary celebration.

The view from the front seat of the Voyage is breathtaking. The 1.2-mile coaster ride is not all sunshine, though. "The Voyage has five underground tunnels—which is a world record," says park president Will Koch, who helped design the ride. "And some of those tunnels are wide enough that the coaster roars through them twice, creating a total of eight underground moments, one of which includes a triple-down feature."

For the design of the Voyage, "We took the traditional out-and-back layout to the extreme," says Will Koch. "With a record three sections of 90-degree banked track, an incredibly steep 66-degree first drop, and a high-energy finish, The Voyage is like no other coaster on the planet."

One of the park's carpenters, Craig Koenig worked on the construction of the Voyage. Notice he is sitting on one of the three sections of 90-degree banked track.

In October 2005, a four-member crew from the Discovery Channel visited Holiday World for five days to shoot construction of the Voyage for their *Building the Biggest: Coaster* television program. As the park's online journal, the HoliBlog, reported, the crew members, from England, Scotland, and New Zealand, proclaimed the new coaster to be "brilliant!"

The Voyage includes three 28-passenger trains to carry coaster lovers on its 1.2-mile adventure through the woods.

"It's our family of hosts and hostesses who make us so special," says Will Koch, who along with his mother, Pat Koch, fully credits their park's seasonal and year-round staff for the World's Friendliest and World's Cleanest awards the park wins year after year. "We tell our hosts and hostesses each spring that we can't rest on last season's laurels; we have to go out and earn those awards again each day. And we'll continue to do that for generations to come!"